D1502303

SCHOOL RECREATION:

Its Organization, Supervision and Administration

BROWN

PHYSICAL EDUCATION SERIES

Edited by

AILEENE LOCKHART
University of Southern California
Los Angeles, California

SCHOOL RECREATION:

Its Organization, Supervision and Administration

J. Tillman Hall

University of Southern California

WM. C. BROWN COMPANY PUBLISHERS
135 SOUTH LOCUST STREET • DUBUQUE, IOWA 52003

KEENE STATE COLLEGE
LIBRARY

LB
3031
. H34

Copyright © 1966
by
Wm. C. Brown Company Publishers

Library of Congress Catalog Card Number: 66-14909

All rights reserved. No part of this book may be
reproduced in any form or by any process without permission in writing from the copyright owner.

64850
KEENE STATE COLLEGE
LIBRARY

Manufactured by WM. C. BROWN CO. INC., Dubuque, Iowa
Printed in U. S. A.

To

Charlie, Edith, Ruth, Mable, Elmore,
Anne, Nancy, George, and Frank Jr.

Preface

There is little doubt that since the beginning of man's existence he has continually sought more time to do with as he wishes. The search has been so gratifyingly rewarded that the question of how to spend the time gained has now become a serious problem. Our schools must and have begun to assume responsibility for providing constructive activities that may be utilized during students' leisure hours — activities that contribute to their over-all growth and development.

Recognition of the values that can be derived from worthwhile school recreational activities has been the major motivation for writing this book. It is believed that carefully selected, organized, and supervised school-sponsored extracurricular activities can pay dividends to the participants and to the school community far beyond usual expectations.

Special appreciation is extended to my wife, Louise, and my daughters, Nancy and Jody, for their help in typing, proofreading, and assembling these materials. Further appreciation is given to Dr. Eleanor Walsh, Dr. Elwood C. Davis, and Dr. Aileene Lockhart for their many contributions. Last but not least, special appreciation is extended to Mrs. Bennie Palmer for her assistance in preparing the final manuscript, and to Cecil Lynch for the photographs.

J. Tillman Hall

Contents

Chapter 1

A Glimpse Into the Past

How long has man inhabited the earth? What is the exact nature of his origin? Answers to these and similar questions may never be known. And yet, the mysterious sometimes is able to be explained to later generations. If geologists and archaeologists have accurately traced the development of man through fossilized remains described by such names as Australopithecus, Java man, Peking man, Neanderthal, Rhodesian, Cro-Magnon, at least we are certain that his evolution has been an extremely slow process.

How long man roamed the valleys, steppes or mountains with little or nothing to cover or shelter his body, we cannot yet say. We can only guess how long he existed without significant speech, without fire to warm his body or to cook his meals or to make the darkness vanish. We do know that he eventually conquered the adversities and hardships of his environment, and that hungry beasts found it more and more difficult to feed on human life.

Scientists have determined that on several different occasions in the past the climate grew steadily colder and more moist. This brought about increasingly heavier snowfalls which were transformed into layers of ice that eventually covered approximately one-sixth of the earth's surface. It is evident that each of these glacial epochs lasted for several thousands of years. The accumulation of ice must have made life almost intolerable for early man. Visualize him, a naked and shelterless being, in the modern sense, with only his bare hands to protect himself and to

1

meet all the necessities of his ever-threatened life. Imagine what he thought, felt, and did.

Despite hardships, man continued to survive, to adjust, and to propagate. Scientists have informed us that the reindeer became one of the greatest aids in primitive man's struggle for life. Reindeer hides were fashioned into clothes, their flesh was used for food, their horns and bones were converted into weapons.

As the climate warmed after the most recent glacial epoch and the ice retreated, Neolithic culture spread over most of the world. This in time gave way to a more modern civilization estimated to have begun about 20,000 years ago. Civilization since then is conveniently marked by the invention of mechanical implements which in time aided man in conquering the darkness and the wilderness. Many ancient man-made articles, ranging from crude stone hatchets to well polished pottery, have been found in caves, on the surface of the earth, and beneath sediment and limestone. These implements, found near man's fossilized remains, make known some of his early activities. Engravings and paintings have also been discovered in caves and rock shelters in France, Spain and Italy. The illustrations inform us of the types of animals man knew and how they were slain. These and other artifacts indicate man's growing mastery of tools and skills which were used during his work and leisure time.

PREHISTORIC MAN

Scientists are in general agreement that man has lived on earth between 500,000 and 1,000,000 years. The oldest written records of man's history, however, date back to about 3,000 years B.C. The long period of man's life prior to the time he learned to write is called prehistory, or prehistoric. Even though prehistoric men did not have cities or writing, it is assumed that they were not without intelligence and that they laid the foundations of civilization. Anthropologists have sketched their existence as follows.

The Old Stone Age extended from man's beginning until about 8,000 years ago. During this time, man invented pebble tools, choppers, hand axes, flake tools, and blade tools. He lived in small groups, many wandering about in search of game, others in permanent settlements, in rock shelters, and in caves.

The New Stone Age began about 6,000 years ago and lasted until 3,000 B.C., the time metals were first invented. During this period, man built permanent villages, learned to farm and herd domesticated animals, and developed specific skills in arts and crafts.

It is assumed man has enjoyed various forms of recreation for many thousands of years. Some information has been discovered by anthropologists and sociologists, although the identity of specific types of recreation is hidden in antiquity. Through a study of ancient stories, fables, legends, pictures, and excavations, the life of prehistoric peoples has been determined in part. They were not concerned with vocational endeavor as it is known to modern man; they took care of life's necessities, nothing more. Their occupations consisted of hunting, meal preparation, fishing, apparel making, shelter building, and moving their belongings from one hunting ground to another. These tasks are examples of the necessities and the adventurous challenges known to exist in primitive man's world. To live demanded creativeness, and indeed creativeness marked man's work until the Industrial Revolution robbed much labor of this quality.

Primeval man's chief purpose was survival. His activities were rigorous and varied enough to make them satisfying, so that, in a sense, recreation was an integral part of work. Adequate food supplies depended upon the ability to discover edible plants, to catch fish, and to kill available wildlife. Many animals apparently did not ignore man as a source of their own food. Considering the crude hunting equipment used by primitive peoples, it is imagined that the contest between man and beast was often a toss-up. How the human race survived as well as it did is still puzzling.

Although prehistoric peoples undoubtedly found the eternal contest with the environment stimulating and at times rewarding, they also engaged in activities that cannot be classified as solely utilitarian. Recent excavations of tombs along the Nile indicate that thousands of years ago children played with crudely-made dolls, tops, marbles, hoops, and other similar objects.

What man did during most of his leisure time must be a mixture of conjecture and interpretation based on the findings of anthropologists and archaeologists. Prior to the beginning of civilization, man probably spent most of his small amount of leisure time as an animal does — sleeping, vegetating, and loafing. There is little doubt that considerable time was spent in dramatizing special happenings into legends and rituals. To modern man, this seems recreational; to primitive man, it was utilitarian.

ANCIENT CIVILIZATIONS

From approximately 6,000 years ago and lasting until 400 A.D. is the period generally classified as ancient times. It included the cultures of

Egypt, Babylonia, Assyria, Persia, Phoenecia, the Hebrews, Greece, and Rome. A study of these bygone civilizations reveals man's slow but continuous progress toward modern civilization.

It is generally believed that the recreational games of these cultures were often imitative of such adult activities as hunting, homemaking, and waging war. There were also many celebrations, rituals, and ceremonies which grew out of literally hundreds of superstitious beliefs. Entire tribes were often brought together during these affairs. It is conceivable that numerous tribal social activities such as dancing, chanting, rhythmic and play activity became a predominant part of these events.

Rituals and ceremonies apparently meant a great deal to ancient man. Anthropologists have indicated that early man's most serious moments probably were those spent in tribal dances. It appears that special dances signified special situations associated with struggles and taboos symbolic of everyday life.

The Cradle of Western Civilization

Civilization began whenever and wherever man settled with a fair degree of permanence and security. To do this, it was necessary to locate places where there was adequate food supply and suitable barriers for protection against the ravages of the environment. The Valley of the Nile, the Tigris, Euphrates, and Indus Rivers were such spots, and here emerged the Egyptian civilization which probably dates back more than 10,000 years.

From whence the Egyptians came has not been definitely established, but their civilization was highly important for it promoted the basic essentials of language, religion, literature, and became the foundation of our Western Civilization.

As man became stabilized in his selected habitat much of his leisure time was spent in improving his way of life. Thus, education and recreation were enmeshed with survival. Embedded in his relatively sheltered home, busy with humble occupations, man perhaps was more peaceful than he had been at any previous time in history.

It is generally believed that leisure time activities during the days of the Egyptians consisted of hunting, fishing, training animals, throwing the spear, and fowling. Some skill was undoubtedly developed in gymnastics, wrestling, and games of low organization. Equipment used for most play activities was of natural origin, thus stimulating imagination, creativeness, and inventiveness.

Ancient Greece

Students of ancient Greece have found that recreation often took the form of physical exercise. The participants engaged in games that were easy to learn; they were regulated by simple rules and were adapted to the city states of the era. Many of the games of low organization currently played by American youth, such as kite-flying, seesawing, tossing games, hide-and-seek, blindman's bluff, and drop-the-handkerchief, were played by Greek youth some three thousand years ago.

Numerous sports seen in the modern Olympic Games stem from Greek origins. The freemen of that nation seem to have participated in recreational activities more extensively than the average American sportsman does today! The list of Greek sports also included swimming, horseback riding, hunting, ball games, chariot races, torch races, rowing, wrestling, boxing, games similar to present-day lacrosse, field hockey, throwing, and numerous kinds of foot races.

The ancient Greeks were beset with appeals to magic, superstition, and sorcery. It appears that even their religion failed. However, their philosophy and the place they gave to recreation survived the disintegration of this once great people.

Ancient Rome

After the Roman legions conquered democratic Greece, they copied many of her recreational pastimes. They failed, however, to absorb Greece's philosophy and attitude toward recreation. In time the Romans became complacent, sedentary, and left active recreation to the slaves and peasants. In time they seem to have become bored with their uncreative, unadventuresome existence. Their amusement consisted of observing paid gladiators who staged bloody death battles.

THE MIDDLE AGES

Between the fall of the Roman Empire and the eleventh century many ideas entered the minds of civilized men. The doctrine of asceticism spread, like a giant plague, from one community to another. Seclusion was the password, and thousands of adults left the confines of society and moved into caves to punish their minds and bodies. Due to self-practiced starvation and uncleanliness, they developed poor mental and physical health and multiple nervous disorders. Education was left in the hands of the monks during the Dark Ages and very little organized recreation was permitted.

THE AGE OF CHIVALRY

Between the eleventh and sixteenth centuries a body of laws, customs, and conventions swept over the western civilized world. Knighthood, the expression of chivalry, was practiced by the upper classes. Major concerns were war, religion, and gallantry. Knighthood tended to foster contempt for the inferior but its contributions to courtesy, honor, and religion helped bring about many of the democratic ideals that we know and practice today.

The training of pages, squires, and knights involved running, wrestling, climbing, hurling stones, swimming, throwing, shooting with the bow, horsemanship, and jousting. Most of these activities are thought of today as physical recreation. It is doubtful if they were so considered by the knights, at least while they were in training.

THE RENAISSANCE AND REFORMATION

Physical activities similar to those engaged in by the knights were the principal recreational outlets during this time. During this period of renaissance, activities were for all and gave the lower classes of people their first sense of freedom in more than a thousand years. It was also in these years that philosophers and writers began to break with tradition and light the candles of freedom which illuminated the pathway to present-day educational thought.

THE EIGHTEENTH AND NINETEENTH CENTURIES

Activities advocated and practiced in Germany, Denmark, and England gave impetus to the recreational movement during the eighteenth and nineteenth centuries. Philosophers and educators emphasized the values of exercise. Physical education began to gain recognition in the school curriculum as did physical recreation as an extracurricular activity. In time, dance, drama, sports, festivals, music, and art became a major part of the cultural pattern.

THE NEW WORLD

The challenges and rigors of frontier existence partially satisfied the recreational desires of the American colonists. Hunting, fishing, house-raising, husking bees, and quilting parties provided the settlers with adequate adventurous, creative, and social outlets. Early inhabitants of the new world found little opportunity for recreation that was not utilitarian as well as enjoyable. The colonists were faced by the wide ocean on one side and the imminently dangerous forest on the other. The ever-impending threat of disease, cold, starvation, and Indian raids forced adoption of uncompromising work regulations. Most of the colonies enacted laws prohibiting many types of amusement. Partly because of the necessity for superior work habits, they condemned recreation and amusement as sinful. In spite of regulations, however, men engaged in pastimes even though faced with criminal punishment when caught.

In time, many of the elemental dangers gradually disappeared, causing a relenting of the restrictions on recreation. Dancing, sleighing, cockfighting, quarter-racing, billiards, bowling, and other types of diversion were customary to some extent in all of the colonies.

Eventually, as the working day shortened, outlets for additional leisure time were needed by the restless, pragmatic Americans. Then came our tremendous sports programs, theaters, musical events, camping, parks, service clubs, "Y's", and countless other agencies and activities to serve the people during their leisure moments.

SIGNIFICANT DEVELOPMENTS IN AMERICAN RECREATION

Consistently through the years, we find an ever-expanding list of leisure-time activities utilized by recreation-minded Americans. Without a doubt, no country in the history of mankind has surpassed America in recreational development. Following are some of the significant landmarks that portray the status of recreation in the past and its rise to its present role in the American way of life.

1565   A plaza established in St. Augustine, Florida. This, in a sense, might be considered the first park land set aside by Colonial settlers.

1611   First recorded game, bowls. This was the first game played by white men in America. It took place in the streets of Jamestown.

1621   Governor William Bradford stopped a primitive game of cricket in Plymouth Colony.

1634   Boston Commons, first city park in the English colonies, was completed.

1640   Ordinance passed by the Massachusetts Bay Colony granting public fishing and hunting rights on all bodies of water that were over ten acres in size.

1657   First published reference to golf in America. Perhaps the game resembled ice or field hockey, for it was first played in the streets.

1665   First mention of organized sport in the United States — horse racing.

1668   First sports trophy awarded. This trophy was made of silver and was given for horse racing. It can be seen in the Yale University Art Center.

1686   First mention of a barefooted game of football.

1716   First theater, Williamsburg, Virginia.

1760   Boston's Faneuil Hall built for musical concerts.

1767   John Street Theater in New York — first permanent theater.

1806   First football game on American soil — played at Yale University.

1820   Several outdoor gymnasiums were erected at different schools
to
1840   and universities.

1823   100,000 witnesses attended a horse race at Long Island.

1825   Round Hill School Gymnasium erected, Northampton, Massa-
        chusetts.

1828   First Archery Club, United Bowmen, Philadelphia.

1844   Professional foot races, called "Pedestrians," were witnessed by
        25,000 people.

1845   Alexander Joy Cartwright drew up the first set of baseball rules.

1846   First baseball game played between the New York Knickerbockers
        and a New York club.

1853   The purchase of land for Central Park in New York City (843
        acres).

1853   Bushnell Park established, Hartford, Connecticut.

1854   Young Men's Christian Association established.

1857   National Education Association established.

1859   First United States Billiard championship.

1859   First intercollegiate baseball game, Amherst vs. Williams College.

1866   Vacation school started in Old First Church of Boston.

1866   Physical education required by law in California Public Schools.

1867   Fairmount Park established, Philadelphia (2,816 acres).

1867   United States Office of Education established.

1868   New York Athletic Club established.

1869   First intercollegiate football game, Princeton vs. Rutgers Uni-
        versity.

1869   First transcontinental railroad completed.

1871   More than 10,000,000 visited New York Central Park.

1871   Rowing Association of American Colleges established.

1872   Kalamazoo Case — compulsory schooling established.

1872   Yellowstone National Park established. Yellowstone National Park
        occupies 2,213,206.55 acres.

1875   IC4A — Intercollegiate Association of Amateur Athletics of America
        — formed.

1876   National Basketball League formed.

1876   National Baseball League formed.

1876   Intercollegiate Football Association formed.

1876   Intercollegiate Track and Field Association formed.

1881   United States Lawn Tennis Association formed.

1885   Boston Sand Gardens formed, the beginning of the accepted recreation movement in the United States.
1885   Association for the Advancement of Physical Education established.
1886   Boston playground provided with professional leadership.
1887   Beginning of settlement house movement, New York City.
1888   Amateur Athletic Union established.
1889   Hull House in Chicago established.
1891   Walter Camp wrote the first book on football.
1892   Boston Metropolitan Park System established.
1895   Big Ten Association established.
1895   First sport pages in newspaper, *New York Journal.*
1897   College Physical Education Association established.
1898   New York City opened school buildings for evening community recreation.
1900   American Baseball League formed.
1903   Harvard built the first football stadium. Chicago South Park District voters approved a five million dollar bond issue to form ten public parks.
1904   Board of Playground ·Commissioners appointed in Los Angeles. Los Angeles was the ·first city to administer recreation under a separate playground commission.
1906   Organization of the Playground Association of America. This became the Playground and Recreation Association of America (1911) and later the National Recreation Association (1930).
1907   First National Recreation Congress. First practical demonstration of the school as a community center building, Rochester, New York.
1910   Boy Scouts of America and American Camping Association were established.
1910   Organized recreation programs were reported to be in operation in 336 cities.
1911   Use of school buildings and grounds for recreation approved by the National Education Association.
1912   Organization of the Girl Scouts and Campfire Girls.
1915   Some 1,157 cities reported they employed full-time recreation leaders.
1916   National Park Service established.
1916   National Community Center Association established.
1919   National Park Association established; first public school camp (Chicago).
1925   Life Camps conducted by Lloyd Sharp.
1932   First International Recreation Congress held, Los Angeles, California.

1933- The following agencies, which greatly aided the development
1936   of recreation, were established: Works Progress Administration,
         Public Works Administration, National Youth Association, and
         Civilian Conservation Corps. The C.C.C., under the National Park
         Service, is said to have advanced the state parks programs by
         some fifty years. These agencies have frequently been referred
         to as Emergency Services Agencies.
1934   American Youth Hostels established.
1938   American Recreation Society organized.
1941   United Service Organization (USO) formed.
1948   Jackson's Mill Recreation Workshop.
1954- Three Professional Preparation of Recreation Personnel national
  56- conferences held.
  62
1959   School Recreation, National Conference, Washington, D.C.

These are but a few of the many stimulating and influential milestones along the path of the recreational movement. As can easily be
seen, recreation is for everyone. It has had a multiple origin from private agencies, schools, municipalities, and federal sponsors. One can
easily see that the recreation movement has come a long way since its
early beginnings. It is generally believed that the schools will play an
increasingly important part in all aspects of tomorrow's recreation
movement.

Chapter 2

Concepts of School Recreation

For the past twenty years, an increasingly large number of schools have added recreation to their offerings. It is almost inconceivable, however, that it has taken so long for recreation to become accepted as a part of the regular school program.

It seems that for generations conformity has enslaved the schools, and that numerous forces have operated to prevent exploration of new approaches to the improvement of education. Also, perhaps the values of recreation appear tarnished by its popularity and commercialization. Many people do not understand the importance of participating in constructive recreational activities.

It is possible, too, that school administrators have been overly sensitive to criticism from the defiant and scornful minority. Pleasurable school activities have brought many derisive remarks from observers who failed to recognize the inherent importance of recreation to the participant. Some seem to be alarmed by what they call the "extravagant" use of leisure time. There is an element of truth in this last statement in certain instances. Perhaps for the present, the following premise is accurate: some people have too much recreation, but the majority have too little.

Let us at this time explore various concepts of recreation. What is it? What theories explain it? What are the accepted beliefs about it?

WHAT IS RECREATION?

The word recreation is derived from the Latin term *recreare*. Its original meaning was to restore, refresh, or build anew. In essence, it

11

referred to some form of action essential to re-creating or revitalizing the individual.

For many years, however, educators have expressed diverse views about the term "recreation." Many have erroneously assumed that recreation, play, amusement, fun, and entertainment are synonymous. This confusion frequently has left the recreation profession in an embarrassing and ambiguous position.

It is true that the words "entertainment" and "amusement" may be used interchangeably as they both refer to agreeably diversified interest. Generally speaking, one thinks of "amusement" as something that is interesting and that temporarily catches the fancy. On the other hand, "entertainment" is thought of as something interesting that is observed, such as a motion picture. The word "fun" refers to laughter-provoking, jovial play. In turn, "play" refers to active, busy movement.

None of the previous definitions adequately defines the term "recreation." Educators have realized tardily that "recreation" is more than whatever a person chooses to do in his own time off the job. This definition was acceptable for a while but is no longer defensible if we expect our recreational programs to be publicly supported. We therefore must subscribe to a definition which encompasses the idea of *acceptable* leisure-time activities. The participant should be expected to become a better individual as a result of his recreational experience. The realization of this aim may be in the development of social, mental, physical, spiritual, or emotional qualities, or a combination of them. The assets must outweigh the deficits of the experience if it is to be called "recreation." Unless a definition incorporating these beliefs is adopted as a rallying point, the recreation movement will continue to be falsely judged.

The term "recreation" need not refer only to those activities undertaken during leisure time. As long as the choice of activity belongs to the participant and the by-product of the experience is rewarding and worthwhile, the activity may be described as recreational.

Recreation, then, is the term used to describe the values derived from any constructive form of play, amusement, entertainment, or relaxation. Recreation includes those things that tend to improve a person and raise him to a higher plane of life. Recreation restores, refreshes, or creates anew socially acceptable qualities.

Recreation need not always be avocational. For some people their recreation may be their vocation, their livelihood. If this is the case, these individuals could be described as being perfectly placed in our society.

Recreation is basically a satisfying of human hungers, a way of living. Recreation is an end unto itself but it also sprinkles dividends of one kind or another in some cases, and pours them in drenching torrents in other situations.

Recreation also may be thought of as an art. No rigid formula is likely to be found to measure accurately its values. This is because recreation depends upon the individual's state of mind and his attitude toward a given activity.

TRADITIONAL THEORIES EXPLAINING PLAY AND RECREATION

Several well known theories have been formulated to explain why people seek recreation. The major traditional theories are the Recreation Theory, the Surplus-Energy Theory, the Instinct-Practice Theory, the Catharsis Theory, the Recapitulation Theory, and the Relaxation Theory.

The Recreation Theory was advanced by Lord Kames, an eighteenth-century English philosopher. The theory implies that recreational activities are necessary for recuperation from the normal wear and tear of everyday life. Recreation provides a change of pace which refreshes both body and mind. It is believed that this theory strongly influenced Guts Muths, the recognized "father of physical education."

The Surplus-Energy Theory, one of the earliest and best known explanations of play, is generally known as the "Schiller-Spencer Theory." Its origin dates back to the last part of the eighteenth century. Its proponents believe play to be an aimless expenditure of surplus energy; some refer to the concept as a "blowing off steam" theory.

The Instinct-Practice Theory was most fully described in the works of Karl Gross at the beginning of the twentieth century. As the title indicates, according to this theory play is believed to result from certain inherited instincts. Play is not only important at the time but serves as training for later life activities.

The Catharsis Theory, probably originated by Aristotle, was developed by Gross, Carr and Claparede and, in general, states that play is a safety valve for pent-up emotions. This theory received strong support in the early years of the twentieth century.

Also early in the twentieth century, G. Stanley Hall wrote enthusiastically about the Recapitulation Theory. Hall contended that play is the result of biological inheritance. The participants, unknowingly, while they play actually recapitulate the "culture epochs" in the development of civilization.

Although not originated by G. T. W. Patrick, the Relaxation Theory seems to have been synthesized by him during the first part of the twentieth century. Patrick suggested that man seeks activities which tend to relieve muscle fatigue and nervous disorders due to involvement in highly skilled and mentally exacting occupations. This theory perhaps is applicable to present-day "urban jitters," referred to as "urbophrenia."

Newer Theories of Play

Several additional theories of play and recreation have been developed. The best known newer theories are Appleton's Physiological Growth Theory, Curtis's Freedom Theory, John Dewey's Learned Responses Theory, L. L. Barnard's Adjustment Complexes Theory, and Harnell Hart's Self-Expression Theory. The latter seems to be the currently accepted theory of why people seek recreational experiences.

Hart's synthesis of twentieth-century thinking on the science of human relations indicates that man is constantly striving to maintain his status. This seems most easily accomplished through self-expression. Man is constantly seeking new experiences through which he can express his integrated personality.

Some have said that recreation has the element of spontaneity, or, in other words the person instantly feels an impelling motive to do something. An analysis of the motive therefore may not always reveal the underlying cause for his action. Frustration, monotony, anxiety, hereditary dispositions, or acquired attitudes may be fundamental causes for many specific actions. There is little doubt that meditation or intuitive musing stimulates considerable activity.

As is the case with most theories, none completely covers all of the possible causes of or motivating factors for recreation. These may not be the same for any two people and they vary from time to time for the same individual. One person may be seeking physical exercise while another seeks companionship. One theory may adequately cover the motivating cause for recreation during one hour, while an entirely different theory may describe the drives which stimulate the same activity at a later time. The motivating cause may not be evident to even the participant.

As we analyze the theories of play and recreation, consider the universal wishes of man, and study the influential patterns of our culture, it becomes evident that human destiny is intimately related to what is done during leisure time. One thing is known for sure: wholesome recreational pursuits provide by-products which can very favorably affect man's future existence.

ACCEPTED BELIEFS ABOUT RECREATION

It is generally believed that recreational motives rank high in the psychological drives of man. Perhaps the desire for security and the sex drive are predominant. Assuming this to be true, the recreational drive could most likely be classified as the third strongest compelling force in the human body.

Recreational interest covers the full span of life. It begins in the cradle and extends to the grave. It includes all subject areas and activities from which plus values can be obtained. Physical education, arts, crafts, music, drama, and countless other subject areas are concerned largely with the development of skills for the worthy use of leisure time.

It becomes, therefore, the school's responsibility to join forces with all other agencies in preparing and planning recreational activities for the improvement of man.

Since the school is generally thought of as the hub of a community, its facilities most appropriate, its leaders best trained, its program highly respected, it should take the lead in organizing youth activities.

Municipal agencies should assist the school in this endeavor. If the school's recreation program is successful, then the municipal program will improve. Unless the school program instills deep-seated interest and develops specific skills, the municipal program may become a humiliating blemish in a community. This is especially true in many large urban districts.

It is most important that the schools not lose sight of their first responsibility, the teaching of fundamental skills. Without skills, recreation loses most of its potential value.

A skilled person will usually find the time and a place to use his skills. The school is the most logical agency to teach most recreational skills, and all facilities possible should be used as a recreational laboratory. Other community agencies should promote supplemental programs which would enrich the entire community.

Chapter 3

The Role of the School in Recreation

In some form or another, school-connected recreation has been found in the United States since Colonial times. At first it existed only as a permissive program, receiving little or no financial assistance. At the present time, however, we find that in many states recreation is encouraged by specific legislation which assures some financial assistance for its organization, supervision, and administration. Some states have established a special school tax, the monies from which are used to conduct leisure-time programs after school hours, during evenings, and on Saturdays, holidays, and during vacation periods. Legislation supporting school recreation falls under headings such as Civic Center Acts, Recreation Enabling Acts, Joint Exercise of Powers Acts, Community Services Acts, and so on. The titles of the legislation differ from state to state, but in most cases the purposes are identical. Such legislation is discussed in Chapter 8.

Historically speaking, school curriculums traditionally have been independent from other community programs and they have followed rather than led in the development of community innovations. This is true particularly in the field of recreation. The role that schools may eventually play in recreation, however, has been suggested by the Los Angeles Metropolitan Recreation and Youth Services Council. This Council recognizes that schools are in a good position to provide for most youth recreational needs. Children are in school for many hours each day. Moreover, the school curriculum makes possible the acquisition of many skills including physical education, music, drama, science, camping, and nature study. Since school plants are centrally located, have extensive recreational facilities, and belong to the citizens of a community, it is believed that the schools are in a key position to develop an understanding of the worthy use of leisure time. Moreover, during the past few years there has been increasing emphasis on adult education. This reflects not only the need for education and the acquisition of professional skills but also interest in recreational pursuits. Large attendance in adult education classes demonstrates that citizens place value on cultural, social, and physical endeavors and look to the schools as a logical place in which to participate in recreational undertakings.

In 1959 the American Association for Health, Physical Education, and Recreation sponsored a national conference on school recreation. Perhaps the most important statements evolving from the conference are in the following list; each received unanimous approval from the delegates who represented all sections of the United States.

1. Schools should educate for the worthy use of leisure.
2. Maximum articulation should be achieved between school instruction and recreation.
3. Schools should coordinate and mobilize the total community resources for recreation.
4. Schools should develop cooperative planning of recreation programs and facilities.
5. Schools should interpret recreation to the people.

Well over 50 per cent of our population now lives in metropolitan areas. Urbanization and automation have forced tremendous sociological, physiological, and psychological problems on all communities: joblessness, shiftlessness, delinquency, neuroticism, borderline misfits. Before the age of buttons and dials, one could expect to obtain at least satisfactory physical release by doing necessary daily chores. This condition no longer exists. As a result, the physical as well as the emotional unfitness of the people of our nation has provoked widespread concern.

Unless the schools stimulate vital interest in wholesome recreational activities, our nation may degenerate. Though some believe that recreation should be left completely to other agencies, many thoughtful persons are convinced that our schools must assume the leading role in developing and maintaining *all* the essentials of a good life. Not to do so would be one of the greatest mistakes the schools could make.

TEACHERS' RESPONSIBILITIES

Teachers must realize that all students need to participate in numerous pleasurable activities. Insofar as possible these should be selected on the basis of their potential educational contribution. By being selective in the recreational activities sponsored by the school, it is possible to alter students' choices of leisure-time pursuits. Though these activities need have little or no utilitarian value, they should contribute to physical fitness, present opportunities for the maintenance of mental balance, teach social graces, provide cultural and creative experiences, and afford opportunities for making new acquaintances. Recreation provides excellent opportunity for aiding in the achievement of normal physical, emotional, and mental growth.

A great deal of teaching can be done outside the classroom. Who is in a better position than teachers to foster *esprit de corps* in students? Without a spirit of pride, no community or nation can achieve its potential. Improvement in the tone of a student body often results from the participation of its members in stimulating recreational pursuits. Many attributes so vainly sought in a direct way can be most easily gained as a by-product of a well administered recreational program. Teachers should remember that at least part of the success of Pestalozzi, Rousseau, and Froebel was due to the fact that they emphasized an interesting recreational approach to education.

Last of all, teachers must be sincere in their beliefs and they must practice what they preach. They should be interesting and interested persons themselves, exemplifying that which they hope to develop in students. They need to be uniquely prepared to guide young, adventurous, and restless minds into exploring and cultivating worthwhile interests and to encourage excellence in daily living. Nothing is more influential than what the student sees.

ADMINISTRATORS' RESPONSIBILITIES

If the school is to transform the leisure-time habits of students into fruitful activities, then the administrator must understand and believe that planned recreation can be an effective device for changing individual behavior. Conflicting and indifferent attitudes exhibited by him toward the total life of students and teachers lead to dissatisfaction and frustration. Life for teachers and students should be more than drudgery and dreams. The administrator should strike the spark that ignites the entire community into purposeful activity, releasing the imagination and determination of others.

By tradition, the administrator is charged with the responsibility of determining the pace of intellectual development of the students in his school. It must be added that he is also responsible for the total growth of all his students and teachers. It is his duty to select teachers, stimulate students, encourage parents, and badger opponents in an effort to put together a winning team. How can he secure maximum growth in all? Coordinating the allied instructional tasks alone is without doubt a staggering problem. But even though the administrator is involved in a multiplicity of additional problems, he is still accountable for the *total* education of all those he manages. Consequently, he must make sure that students are guided into all experiences that can strengthen them physically, intellectually, socially, and emotionally. If he takes an eagle's-eye view of his responsibilities, he will recognize the unlimited contributions a good school recreation program can provide.

THE SCHOOLS' RESPONSIBILITY

With leaders of vision using efficient methods, our luxury-loving children can be stimulated to creative interests. This will be no easy task, as many have become captives of television and material ease; many are undisciplined and emotionally overindulged. Some are overly aggressive, while others are either spongelike or irresponsible.

Even though in many ways we are the most advanced nation in the history of the world, present physical inactivity and poor emotional outlets will without doubt eventually slacken the mental processes of a large number of our people. The schools must ardently champion wholesome activity. Seeds basic to the development of rational and healing activity must be planted and carefully cultivated.

How can the schools devote additional time to organizing and administering a dynamic educational recreation program? Additional *qualified* staff must be employed. Every school should have professional personnel who work afternoons, evenings, and weekends. Recreational experiences are so valuable that they warrant professional supervision as does any other laboratory experience.

A good recreation program would probably keep in school a great many of the million dropouts each year. These jobless and placeless individuals become drifters, rejects, and shiftless teen-agers. Many of them are in trouble and constitute social dynamite.

The schools cannot afford not to assist our youth in their inalienable right to enrich and develop their personalities to the fullest. Crash programs designed to meet the crises of the moment are not the answer. We must increase the amount and quality of leisure-time leadership at all levels of our educational ladder. This is necessary if we are to accomplish the things that we know are possible through school recreation.

From a meager beginning, we have seen that recreation has risen to a prominent place in some schools but deserves more widespread acceptance. Educators are now recognizing the cluster of values that tend to arise from wholesome leisure-time experiences. Citizens are aware that the schools receive a large share of the tax dollar, that extensive and expensive facilities are unused late afternoons, evenings, Saturdays, and holidays. They expect the schools to develop within students lifelong interests, attitudes, and skills. Schools now must lead in encouraging and providing sound recreational programs for all communities.

Chapter 4

The Values of School Recreation

The first time recreational activities became a part of the school program is not known; neither is it known at what stage in history the first schoolhouse was constructed. The answers would be most interesting; however, they are not essential in the development of the thesis of this book. It is assumed that various forms of recreational programs have existed in numerous schools for a long time.

In this chapter we are concerned basically with the development of values as they can be derived from a well developed school recreation program.

VALUES

The term "value" is sometimes abstract and at other times concrete. In a sense, it is used as a synonym for "worth" or "goodness." It is an ambiguous term often possessing both objective and subjective qualities. Value is placed on something as the result of judgment, and it involves both extrinsic and intrinsic qualities.

It would be virtually impossible to assign an exact value to every recreational experience. Nevertheless, specific values can be assumed even though accurate measuring techniques may never be discovered. The world will never reach the stage where everything can be objectively measured. Love, friendship, respect, enjoyment, and many other qualities are intangibles and so are many of the values of recreation; thus, their precise worth must be based upon educated guesses.

It has been partly through an external value system that our great country, founded upon individual enterprise, has been developed. Many of the values by which we live are, therefore, external, based upon external achievements. This is not necessarily as it should be and it has left us, in the eyes of many, culturally deficient.

Sometimes we behave as if happiness were dependent on technological development. This attitude may eventually be our downfall as a nation. As a result of industrial advances, man actually may be losing the deep-seated satisfaction that comes from creativity. Devotion to the accumulation of material wealth by means of robot-like effort leaves little room for wholesome recreational interest. Physiological, psychological, and sociological research indicates the need for recreational outlets. All ages can derive immeasurable values from absorbing recreational interests. Whether it be for the release of pent-up emotions, the freeing of the mind, the exercise of the muscles, or the comradeship that is developed, recreation must be recognized as being invaluable to mankind.

Those in administrative capacities in education must not shrink from their responsibility. They must make sure that each school has a dynamic recreational program. They must understand that attributes sought by direct means in many instances can be more easily obtained as by-products of wholesome recreation. Young people often are caught in a mesh of desires and passions that demand outward expression. Recreational activities properly supervised can bring these under control. Unless someone understands and does something about them, the attempts to satisfy these deep-seated needs may have tragic results.

Schools have been urged to increase the number of required courses in mathematics and science. The pressure for these changes has been so strong that many other fields have lost favor and are looked upon as being secondary in importance. It appears that everyone is either being prepared to build spaceships or to pilot them. Some understanding of science and mathematics is needed by everyone, but these are not the only important disciplines. There are many other subjects and activities that merit attention.

The greatest natural resource is the youth of our nation. Everything possible should be done, therefore, to assure their proper development. Recreational activities afford excellent opportunities for developing desirable attitudes, learning worthwhile skills, and enjoying a pleasurable and meaningful life.

Physiological Values of Recreation

Most authorities agree that physical activity is conducive to optimum physical growth. The student of recreation needs a general understanding of human physiology and of the muscular system in particular in order to appreciate certain by-products of physical recreation. Although these topics cannot be discussed adequately within the scope of this book, it seems appropriate to indicate some of the physiological benefits of physical recreation.

In general, research has shown the following benefits of physical recreation:

1. Exercise is essential in the development of physical structure and function. Activity tends to develop a strong, well coordinated, flexible body.
2. Daily physical recreation generally assists in the attainment of vitality, endurance, and resistance to fatigue.
3. Recreation relieves the nervous tension brought on by normal daily routine and helps to prevent functional nervous disorders.
4. Neuromuscular training through physical activities coordinates muscles and nerves. Thus, the trained individual is able to conserve nervous energy.
5. Physical recreation is one of the best forms of rest and relaxation.
6. Physical recreation can improve body mechanics.
7. The circulation of blood as well as lymph is accelerated by exercise.
8. Kinesthetic perception can be improved through the practice of motor skills.
9. Play sometimes rests visual and auditory organs.
10. Exercise hastens the removal of waste material.
11. Exercise induces deeper breathing.
12. Exercise develops the large muscles, increases blood circulation, and promotes the digestion of food.

Psychological Values of Recreation

The human personality is a complicated mechanism. Psychologists, educators, and parents have long attempted to discover what attributes are essential to the development of an integrated personality. What is it that makes a well balanced individual? What experiences contribute to the development of desired qualities?

In the judgment of some of our best educators, specific psychological values can be derived by participating in wholesome recreational activities, for example:

1. Human behavior is impelled by forces felt in the form of *wishes*, such as the wish for recognition, the wish for security, the wish for new experiences, and the wish for response. All of these desires can be satisfied to some degree by participating in wholesome recreational activities.

2. Second-order drives such as curiosity, gregariousness, self-assertion, self-abasement, and imitativeness can most likely be satisfied through participation in recreation.
3. Through play and recreation, an individual often learns personal worth, secures status and acceptance, maintains personal integrity, and develops good social relationships.
4. Through recreational activities young people can learn to think, anticipate, and interpret the laws of cause and effect.
5. Recreation affords the opportunity for that very important personal satisfaction, success. Through frequent successful experiences a person develops self-confidence, overcomes timidity, and finds happiness in his achievements.
6. Recreation can assist in developing qualities such as honesty, fair play, leadership, resourcefulness, followership, self-control, self-confidence, poise, originality, perseverance, and personal courage.
7. Recreation affords excellent opportunities for releasing aggression in a socially acceptable manner.
8. Recreation can be very important to mental health.
9. A variety of recreational interests can prevent excessive daydreaming.
10. Recreation offers opportunities for a balance between dependence and independence.
11. Recreation can assist in maintaining a high level of resiliency.
12. Recreation provides challenging situations and opportunities which aid in growth toward emotional maturity.
13. Recreational activities offer opportunities for social interaction, cooperation, and competition.

Sociological Values of Recreation

Any wholesome activity that tends to develop better human understanding, cooperation, tolerance, and neighborliness is certainly worthy of public support. Recreation affords opportunities for all of these, for example:

1. Characteristics such as courtesy, fair play, and good sportsmanship can be by-products of well supervised recreation.
2. Social development is greatly advanced through recreation. It is believed that desirable attitudes such as helpfulness, kindness, truthfulness, justice, and general constructive behavior are by-products of a good recreational experience.
3. Through recreational activities participants have an opportunity to exchange views, attend numerous social functions, discover new interests and friends, and in general mature properly.

4. Recreational activities help reinforce the individual's efforts to attain selfhood, to gain purpose, and to reach self-set goals.
5. Recreational activities can help an individual to feel secure, strong, and capable of self-direction, even though home life may be disturbed.
6. Recreation affords an opportunity for many to excel. Students who are unable to excel in scholastic endeavors may achieve a feeling of success through participation in school recreation.
7. A person's personality tends to mature and his behavior becomes more acceptable when he learns to compete successfully in recreational activities.
8. Participation in recreational activities increases a person's ability to make correct judgments.
9. The matching of skill, endurance, and strategy against others in recreational activities tends to add zip and enthusiasm to one's life.

It is recognized that the preceding lists give only a sample of the countless physiological, psychological, and sociological values which may accrue from recreational experiences. Certainly it is safe to say that the combined values contribute toward living a more enjoyable and fruitful life.

The chart on page 26 presents a summary of the rewards of participation in worthwhile recreational pursuits which have been mentioned in this chapter.

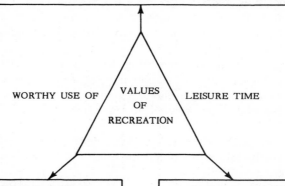

PSYCHOLOGICAL VALUES

1. Relieves neuro-muscular tension.
2. Develops appreciation, values, attitudes.
3. Develops self-expression and discipline.
4. Develops inquiring mind.
5. Improves emotional control.
6. Stimulates esthetic interests.
7. Develops personality.
8. Develops courage, fortitude, and resiliency.
9. Develops sportsmanship.
10. Affords opportunity for response and recognition.
11. Greatest opportunity for joyous activity.
12. Improves analytic thinking.
13. Develops insight.
14. Opportunity to develop worthwhile interest and hobbies.
15. Develops determination and a willingness to sacrifice.
16. Provides background for serenity, sanity, and cheerfulness.

WORTHY USE OF

VALUES
OF
RECREATION

LEISURE TIME

SOCIOLOGICAL VALUES

1. Develops democratic attitude.
2. Develops respect and tolerance.
3. Worthy use of leisure time.
4. Develops fellowship and leadership.
5. Gives opportunity for new experiences.
6. Improves family and community ties.
7. Medium for social integration.
8. Develops group loyalties and responsibilities.
9. Beneficial to the improvement of scholarship.
10. Develops a sense of belonging.
11. Develops group consciousness.
12. Contributes to character development.
13. Contributes to moral and spiritual values.
14. Contributes to community solidarity.
15. Develops a respect for community property.

PHYSIOLOGICAL VALUES

1. Improves safety skills.
2. Remedial and preventive.
3. Develops organic vigor, power, strength, endurance, respiratory and circulatory efficiency, and muscle tone.
4. Increases flexibility, speed, and general coordination.
5. Improves kinesthetic sense.
6. Develops a state of sound vitality.
7. Develops increasing recreational skills.
8. Develops habits of personal cleanliness.

Figure 4.1

26

Chapter 5

Leadership, the Key to the Program

Leadership is generally defined as the ability to stimulate, guide, and direct others; if it is constructive leadership the direction is desirable and approved by the group. A leader has influence because others follow him and his advice.

How does leadership in recreation compare with leadership in other professions? The basic qualities that characterize the recreation leader are essentially those that personify the leader in any other profession. Not everyone agrees with this statement. Some believe that the better recreation leaders are more democratic in their leadership than are those in some other professions. Be that as it may, democratic leadership is essential to good recreational leadership; the autocratic recreation leader generally has trouble developing sustained interest in his program. If he is hesitant in or incapable of making immediate decisions, however, neither he nor his program will be popular but the most successful recreation leaders do use the democratic approach whenever they have opportunity to do so.

IS LEADERSHIP ABILITY INHERITED?

It is a recognized fact that leaders rather quickly stand out from others. They often have striking appearance, are healthy, bold, and are superior in school work and fluency of speech. Generally speaking, leaders are taller, heavier, better looking, more athletic, more intelligent, and more independent than nonleaders. Once leadership is attained, it appears to be a lasting characteristic. Though physical attributes such as size are largely hereditarily determined, other qualities appear to be learned. Such attributes as temperament, personality, initiative, persistence, and ability to deal with people are acquired. Most of the learned qualities necessary for successful leadership have their foundation in childhood and adolescence and are the result of numerous successful experiences.

WHY RECREATIONAL LEADERSHIP?

There are numerous reasons why leadership is needed in recreation. Americans on the whole dislike solitude, and the need for leadership grows in proportion to the number of individuals who find themselves in a group. Our fast-growing population has shifted from rural to urban habitation. In this location there is little opportunity for an individual to initiate his own recreation. Day by day, there is less outdoor space available for active recreational pursuits. The ever-expanding metropolis makes it virtually impossible for most teen-agers to enjoy natural recreation such as hunting, fishing, or exploring the diminishing fields and forests.

Leadership is needed because of the ever-increasing amount of free time. Many daily chores have been eliminated because we have gas and electric energy, running water, power mowers, dishwashers, canned and packaged food, vacuum cleaners, fast transportation, supermarkets, deep freezers, and countless other innovations. Kaplan estimates that a man now

has about 45,000 free hours to do with as he pleases during his lifetime (35:12). This means that, based upon a life span of seventy years, a person has, on the average, six and one-half hours of leisure time each day. In all likelihood, the coming generation can not depend upon work to give meaning to their lives. If this be true special training will be required to live harmoniously with tomorrow's leisure. Unfortunately certain recreational activities that once were attractive now seem to have lost appeal for our youth. In some instances, however, old activities have come to seem new and invigorating merely because they have been glamorized. Some good examples are Little League Baseball, Pop Warner Football, and touring amateur dance troups such as the Westchester Lariats.

Tension is rapidly becoming man's greatest killer. It often results from unsolved problems, continuous frustrations, prolonged worry, anxiety, irritability, confusion about purposes, the hum of the city, and the ever-increasing tempo of life in general. Without doubt, tension in coming generations will increase. Authorities agree that the best release is by participating in regularly scheduled recreation for this has a "grounding" influence on pent-up emotions, a known therapeutic value.

School Recreation Leaders

Several titles other than the more general one of "recreation leader" are customarily used to refer to individuals associated with school recreation work. The term "recreation educator," for example, often designates a college or university teacher who is responsible for the professional preparation of future recreation leaders. In many situations the recreation educator may also be responsible for on-campus recreation programs. In other words, a part of his work load is in teaching, the other in supervision and planning. The majority of college and university programs are handled in this manner.

Under such an arrangement, the recreation educator, or "recreation director," has numerous assistants, either paid or voluntary, who do most of the face-to-face leadership. His responsibility and duties thus fall primarily in the realm of coordination, in-service training, supervision, and policy-making.

The same general work plan often prevails in the public schools where the recreation leader also may be called the "recreation director." Most of the recreation directors in public schools teach at least half of the time. The remainder of their time is allocated to supervising the school recreation program.

The high school or college teacher responsible for recreation is sometimes also referred to as the "recreation administrator" or "coordinator of recreation." In other instances, no special title distinguishes this person from his colleagues in other fields. The duties and responsibilities of the administrative head of the recreation department differ, of course, from one school to another, depending upon a number of variables such as objectives, organization, size and location of the school.

Persons responsible for either school or college recreation are extremely dependent upon another type of leader, the "volunteer." It is essential that these people be selected carefully and conscientiously prepared before they assume leadership positions. One ineffective, unqualified recreation leader can thwart, confuse, and upset the entire program. The volunteer leader should have most of the personal qualities outlined throughout this chapter.

Special counseling, in-service training, and guidance should be given every volunteer leader. The work of volunteers should be regularly evaluated by the supervisor, preferably by personal observation. Leaders also should be given several self-evaluating techniques by which they can determine their progress.

It is essential that volunteer leaders receive adequate recognition and commendation for each worthy performance. They are entitled also to a sense of belonging and all of the other benefits generally bestowed on those in a similar position. It is well to remember that at the present time the volunteer leader is the very backbone of the school recreation program Eventually the schools probably will be in position to employ many recreation directors and educators. Until that time, the program must rest partly in the hands of volunteer leaders.

RECRUITMENT OF RECREATIONAL PERSONNEL

Perhaps the greatest problem facing the recreation profession lies in the recruitment of adequate personnel. Why are so few students interested in majoring in recreation? There are numerous reasons, some of which follow.

Many simply do not know that a person can major in recreation or have little or no knowledge about its opportunities. We have not adequately encouraged boys and girls to enter the profession. There has not been sufficient promotion and participation in career conferences by present recreation personnel. Sufficient printed materials pointing out the values in this profession are lacking. High school counselors, because of lack of information, do not think to guide potential leaders in this direction.

Some thoughtful students do not consider recreation as a profession because they have heard such allegations as the field is loaded with uninspired leadership, the profession tolerates inferior standards of work, and the professional curriculum is inadequate. Some have heard that adequate counseling, student aid, scholarships, fellowships, assistantships and in-service training are unavailable to prospective students of recreation. Some are told that the salary prospects are not attractive.

The prospective student should be assured, however, that most of the foregoing assertions are not true and that there are unlimited opportunities for excellent placement after graduation. The graduate may choose to go into municipal recreation, American Red Cross work, industrial recreation, school recreation, camping, youth work with such organizations as the YMCA and YWCA, armed forces recreation, Scouting, aquatics, Peace Corps, commercial recreation, or a host of other positions. Today's young people are searching for something meaningful to do with their lives. Perhaps they will not overlook the aspect of service to humanity as did many of their fathers whose aim in too many cases was directed mainly toward high-paying positions.

Qualities and Attributes of a Recreation Leader

It would be almost impossible to list all of the qualities desired in the recreation leader. The difficulty of possessing or developing all of these attributes can be seen. Still, it is essential that a recreation leader *try to become* the best leader possible. The following list is not necessarily complete but does include many highly desired qualities.

1. *Health.* It is paramount that the leader be in good health. Otherwise he is likely to lack stamina, endurance, vitality, drive, and emotional stability. A leader's poor health adversely affects those he leads. The wise leader will recognize the fact that ideas do not come to a man who is worn out. He therefore will make sure he gets adequate rest and reserve time for himself. Even cows and wells run dry.
2. *Imagination.* The leader should have intelligence, foresight, ingenuity, initiative, resourcefulness, and above-average originality, but he should know when to pretend ignorance and when to conceal his wisdom. He should be imaginative and able to initiate those actions he deems worthwhile. This often requires an attitude of "knowing that you can do it." The leader must be a hustler. He should not be afraid to take risks and to assume responsibility. He must be a salesman and must have the gumption to promote his beliefs.
3. The intelligent leader will be aware that if he does not use his talent he will lose it. He should have the ability to analyze, synthesize, explain, deduce, and generalize. Obviously the good leader will use his intelligence to acquire sufficient professional knowledge.
4. *Friendliness.* An unsurpassed interest in the people he serves is a requirement for a good recreation leader. Friendliness tends to develop school and community solidarity. People are generally more coopera-

tive with their friends and receptive to their ideas. Remember the old saying, "If you ride a horse, sit close and tight; if you ride a man, sit easy and light."

5. *Flexibility*. Flexibility is a youthful trait. Those who are to lead youth should seek new and stimulating methods of doing so. The leader should display both versatility and adaptability, for these are essential in most democratic situations.

6. *Aggressiveness*. While having confidence in himself the leader must be conscious of his limitations. His aggressiveness and self-assertion should not be allowed to become offensive to those he leads. He should attempt to make all tasks "do-able." He should prepare the way before issuing a directive and should beware of swimming against the current. Most of all, he should strive to have all things done well. He must maintain the ability to remain cool under fire.

7. *Integrity*. Great leaders have a reputation for standing by their word. They are basically honest and live by an acceptable set of principles. They are capable of thinking independently and are cognizant of the fact that the majority is not always right. When things go wrong, the superior leader blames himself, the inferior leader blames others. The leader must be trustworthy, reliable, and always remember that if he cannot obey, he cannot direct.

8. *Enthusiasm*. One of the first attributes of a good recreation leader is enthusiasm. He should have an infectious spirit that stimulates interest. He must have an imagination that inspires, a vision that guides and the enthusiasm that stimulates others. Great leaders have often made enthusiastic statements which became rallying cries: "Give me liberty or give me death"; "Make the world safe for democracy"; "We have nothing to fear but fear itself"; "Damn the torpedoes! Full speed ahead"; "Remember the Alamo"; "We shall fight on the beaches, we shall fight on the landing grounds, we shall fight in the fields and in the streets, we shall fight in the hills, we shall never surrender"; "I have nothing to offer but blood, toil, tears, and sweat"; "We have not yet begun to fight"; "Ask not what your country can do for you, but what you can do for your country." Yes, enthusiasm electrifies. Generally speaking, a Paul Revere ride — if the cause is worthy — will turn the tide. The enthusiastic leader is a "go-getter"; he challenges others and likes to be challenged himself.

9. *Attractiveness*. The good recreation leader makes himself attractive. He must be alert and look the part of the leader. This is done, at least partially, by developing good posture, by being neat, appropriately dressed, clean and properly groomed, by displaying good manners, and by being sincerely courteous.

10. *Pleasing Personality*. Personality is an ambiguous term but, as used here, it may be thought of as a composite of all the qualities, features, and traits that an individual possesses, or it may be considered to be "an individual's characteristic reaction to social stimuli." A "pleasing personality" describes a person who genuinely likes and is liked by people. Often such a person is cheerful, sympathetic, tactful, patient, tolerant, diplomatic, and has a good sense of humor. Sometimes he is described as having a sunny disposition. Personality is based upon inherited characteristics and learned patterns. In other words, it is the result of a long process of growth based on original potentiality.

There are numerous external characteristics of personality which strongly influence first impressions. They are dress, voice, posture, gestures, manners, motor coordination, and facial expression. It is essential that the recreation leader get off to a good start. He should therefore pay close attention to all of these external factors. It is true that in time their influence with well-known acquaintances wears off. These characteristics are, however, very important in making a favorable first impression.

Often prestige and status are vital factors in maintaining an integrated personality. These are gained from such varied sources as position, rank, office, good fortune, achievement, dress, recognition, and reputation. Status is based on an evaluation of a person's behavior by his associates.

There are qualities and characteristics which can be developed which are associated with a favorable personality: altruism, understanding, sympathy, dependability, integrity, wide interests, conversational ability, and personal appearance. Qualities not associated with a favorable personality include egocentricity, exhibitionism, dishonesty, fear, anger, jealousy, infantilism, physical handicaps, lack of understanding, and overestimation of one's importance. A reminder of the latter is the story about the fly sitting on the coach wheel saying, "See what dust I make."

11. *Maturity*. Growing up partly means growing wiser in mind and stronger in character. Certainly it is desirable for the leader to be more mature than those he leads. A person is maturing properly when his power over his environment is matched by an awareness of what is involved in what he does. If power of execution forges ahead while power of understanding lags behind, maturation is incomplete. One definition of maturity given by Webster refers to pottery. Someone has cleverly extended this to personal maturity. Mature pottery, the analogy goes, is pottery that has been fired to its greatest strength; the mature leader is one who has developed to his optimum ability.

Many additional qualities believed to be desirable in the recreation leader could be listed, but those suggested are essential in leadership.

THE DEVELOPMENT OF LEADERS

What things are influential in the development of a leader? The following list, derived from research results, summarizes important influences:

1. *Family Life.* Advice, strong direction, and a keen interest on the part of one or both parents.
2. *Education.* A broad general education through the college level, preferably in smaller private schools, and a sound professional education in the chosen field.
3. *Religion.* A strong personal religion and an understanding and appreciation of other religions.
4. *Reading.* Exposure to good books and an interest in and appreciation of them.
5. *Travel.* Extensive travel experiences, both local and world-wide.
6. *People.* Opportunities to meet and know many local, national, and international leaders in all fields.
7. *Organizations.* Membership, participation, and leadership experiences in Youth organizations (YMCA's, Boy Scouts, 4-H Clubs, etc.); church organizations, youth and adult; school and college organizations; community organizations (PTA, Kiwanis, Masons, etc.).
8. *Sports and Recreation.* Participation in worthy and carefuly selected sports and leisure-time activities.

PRINCIPLES OF RECREATION LEADERSHIP

Principles are generally thought of as foundational guides or rules for action. They may evolve from considered opinion, widely accepted belief, or authenticated facts.

Every profession must be guided by sound principles if its endeavors are to be successful; indeed it could not claim professional status otherwise. In school recreation, the leader must refer continually to the principles of his field for assistance. We have previously noted that the leader usually is termed a "director" or "supervisor"; this is because he not only provides face-to-face leadership but is responsible for coordinating and supervising numerous activities in which volunteer leadership is both customary and essential. This complex assignment would be very difficult if there were no guiding principles.

The following principles are representative of those which determine the practices of the effective school recreation director, or supervisor.

1. The reciprocal relationship which exists between the school and its supporting community should be understood and appreciated.
2. School recreation should be looked upon as more than merely having a good time.
3. Understanding and concern for each staff member's and participant's welfare is important and must be sincere.
4. Cooperative teamwork should be sought.
5. All personnel should be used in accordance with their capacities.
6. All parts of each job must be understood so that new leaders and as well as those already at work can be assisted and properly supervised.
7. Staff members should be kept well-informed.
8. Responsibilities should be carefully and wisely delegated.
9. Facilities, leaders and opportunities should be made available to all participants.
10. Planning should be realistic, within the limits of budget allowances, available leadership and facilities.
11. Personnel adequately trained in first aid procedures should always be available.
12. Creativity and efficiency should be sought and encouraged.
13. Decisions and actions should be fair and impartially made.
14. Decisions should be sound and timely and full responsibility for each should be assumed.
15. All meetings should be conducted in a diplomatic manner.
16. A spirit of group cooperation and mutual purpose should be sought.
17. Desirable attitudes toward all community endeavors should be maintained.
18. Internal motivation rather than external stimulation should be encouraged.
19. Freedom of expression without fear of reprisals should be expected.
20. Leadership in others should be developed by giving them opportunities to lead.
21. Current knowledge of the learning process should guide leaders in presenting new activities.
22. Leaders should provide direction.
23. Rivalry should be used cautiously and only as a motivating technique.
24. Leaders should have knowledge about and understanding of the participants they serve.
25. Recreational leaders should operate under the assumption that play is universal and never outgrown.
26. Leaders should help youth learn that they cannot always win and winning is not always of the greatest importance.

27. Some success for each participant should be assured, for a series of defeats for an awkward or insecure youth can be very harmful.
28. Security, recognition and status should be sought for all staff members and participants.
29. Leaders should be alert to needs of individuals as well as groups.
30. Professional appearance should be expected at all times (well-groomed, well-mannered, and well-prepared).
31. Attention in most cases should be directed to the majority rather than the few.
32. The participant's personality should be respected at all times.
33. Leadership should be managed in such a way that followers are least conscious of being led.
34. The program should be started on a small scale and then expanded in relation to participants' desires.
35. Active rather than spectator participation should be encouraged.
36. The program should be broad, including a variety of club and craft activities, sports and athletics, social and cultural activities.
37. All aspects of the program should be conducted for the betterment of mind, body and spirit.
38. The program should be organized and conducted directly in relation to the community it serves.
39. The program should provide leadership for all colors, creeds and economic levels.
40. The participant's health and safety should always be protected.
41. Opportunities for social development should be created and fostered.
42. Parental interest and participation should be encouraged.
43. Some proficiency should be sought, for appreciation and joy in an activity requires some mastery of it.
44. The program should include activities for both sexes and all ages.
45. Activities should be terminated with a feeling of accomplishment.
46. Provision for recreation for the handicapped should be made.
47. Credit and praise should be given when and where due.
48. Commendation should be given publicly, reproof privately.
49. Criticism should be constructive.
50. Proof of successful leadership should be sought in the results obtained.
51. Practices and policies should be reviewed often to see that they are appropriate and fair to all.
52. Observations and check sheets should be used only in conjunction with a follow-up conference between the supervisor and the person being evaluated.
53. All facets of the program should be studied and appraised.

54. The outcomes of the program should be the greatest concern.
55. A spirit of happiness should pervade throughout the total school recreation program.

These are but a few of the many principles to which a good recreation leader must subscribe. Sound principles should be used as guides from which the recreation program evolves.

CHALLENGES TO THE RECREATION LEADER

During the past few decades an ever-increasing number of complex forces have been actively functioning on the American scene. Many say that these adversely affect the personality and culture of Americans and that the effect on leisure-time pursuits is unparalleled in history. Perhaps the most baffling aspect is that all of these forces seem to have unfolded at approximately the same time. Thus it is not the solving of one problem that challenges us, but the disentangling of numerous interrelated problems.

What are the forces that seem to be changing our way of life? To review, they include industrialization which reduces creativity; automation which enlarges our knowledge but substitutes machines for men; increased concentration of population which has necessitated unaccustomed ways of living; increased population which is rapidly becoming a major world problem; birth control methods which can aid the cause of planned parenthood; food preservation methods which can lessen world problems; atomic energy which can either destroy the world or become its greatest discovery; better education and higher standards of living which have considerably broadened our horizons; miracle drugs which have noticeably increased longevity; rapid transportation which is rapidly shrinking our world; advances in communication; a trend toward socialism as a result of which we have Social Security, pensions and old-age benefits; and increased leisure time leaving thousands of hours to be profitably or destructively used.

Recreation leaders need to understand the results of these forces and should attempt to see that the problems and opportunities which they have brought about are transformed into fruitful experiences.

One of the great challenges for the remainder of this century probably will be to keep man constructively and actively engaged. The recreation leader's responsibility is obvious. The school recreation director is in a position to help develop lifetime habits and attitudes. Never did the world need more imaginative and wise leadership.

Chapter 6

Administration

It is recommended that the administrator of a school recreation program be carefully selected and then given broad executive responsibilities. He should be authorized and charged with planning, organizing, managing, directing, controlling, and evaluating every phase of the program. In general, he should also be held answerable for the failure or success of every project.

It is doubtful if any school program exceeds that of recreation in scope and in diversity of contributions to student welfare. It therefore is necessary to analyze some of the qualifications, responsibilities, and procedures of the recreation administrator.

QUALITIES OF THE RECREATION ADMINISTRATOR

The personal qualities desired in a director of school recreation do not necessarily differ from those listed in Chapter 5. Ideally speaking, the more of these qualities possessed, the better the chance of succeeding as an administrator. Perhaps it is helpful, however, to list separately a few of the most essential characteristics of the administrator as indicated by authorities.

The administrative head should possess certain specific qualities. The following list is drawn heavily from the work of Hughes, French and Lehsten (32:33-34).

1. He should display the type of leadership that would favorably influence the growth of recreation in the school.

2. He should possess the ability and desire to work with others.
3. He should have adequate educational background as well as practical experience.
4. He should have certain convictions based on continual evaluation of values and sound judgment.
5. He should encourage the staff to take an active part in making decisions and determining policy.
6. He should inform the staff that the decisions which he has had to make prior to the time the staff itself arrived at an agreement are only temporary in nature. Thus, he always leaves the door open for further considerations.
7. He should guide or lead his staff in a manner beneficial to the group.
8. He must originate ideas and assist in coordinating and implementing the ideas of others.
9. He must display patience and willingness to wait for acceptance of recommended changes.

Havel and Seymour listed the following qualities, among others, which they deem essential in equipping the administrator for his post (31:12-15).

1. He should possess broad vision and cognizance of the relationships between his department and other departments in the school and the community.
2. He should have adequate academic preparation, personal qualifications, and profound experience.
3. He should have an excellent understanding of the goals and purposes of health education, physical education and recreation, as well as the broad field of education.
4. He should possess a broad academic background and an insight into the process of human relationships as they influence our society.
5. He should possess effective communicative skills.
6. He should have a dynamic personality, coupled with an abundance of practical intelligence.
7. His attitude must foster confidence and respect among his associates.
8. He should have a well-rounded point of view that includes convictions regarding the dignity of his profession and the dignity of man.

Forsythe and Duncan (28:80) listed additional responsibilities and requisites, such as:

1. The administrator is responsible for the development of high staff morale.
2. The administrator must be available to all staff members and should not show favoritism to any individual.

3. The administrator should strive to develop all the areas within the department to the maximum.

In summary, the administrator should have all the qualities and attributes of a great teacher, and then more. The morale, influence, and reputation of his department with the students, faculty, school, and community are dependent upon the decisions and impressions he makes at every turn of the road. It is therefore essential that he have personal and professional integrity, good mental and physical health, contagious enthusiasm, productive energy, and an understanding of nature and needs of people — their motivations, aspirations, strengths, and weaknesses. The director should be able to manage people and facilities with dignity and efficiency.

PRINCIPLES OF ADMINISTRATION

When we talk about the principles of administration, we are referring to recommended practices based upon the best information currently known. Application of these principles results in the best ways of organizing, promoting, supervising, and managing a school recreation program. These principles will be put into action as the administrator studies, observes, and experiences actual administrative work. Authors (31:6-9; 32; 9; 16; 26) inconsistently suggest that the administrator abide by such principles as the following:

1. The first principle of administration is that of central but delegated responsibility (line and staff organization).
2. The duties and responsibilities of each staff member should be clearly defined and made so that individuals and their abilities complement and supplement each other.
3. Specific authority and responsibilities should be delegated to the staff; then these persons should be expected and allowed to carry out these duties and given full authority to do so.
4. Specialists and specific divisions within the department should serve as parts of the whole rather than as independent units.
5. Each member of the staff should be encouraged to take an active part in all administrative decisions and to contribute to the development of all aspects of the program. This principle is that of democracy in action.
6. Administrative decisions should always be made in accordance with the principle of consistency, that is, in accordance with established policies.
7. The principle of efficiency requires that fullest and best use be made of all personnel and facilities.

8. It should always be possible to be flexible in dealing with unforeseen problems.
9. There should be an equitable distribution of funds, time and attention.

ADMINISTRATIVE POLICIES

After principles have been established, policies come next. When we refer to the administrative policies of school recreation programs, we are talking about the wise conduct of the complete program. Desirable policies are based upon sound principles.

Administrative planning will involve the establishment of policies about the following: school-community relationships, opportunities for democratic experiences, prevention of accidents, juvenile delinquency and other problems; finance, administration, supervision, and leadership in all phases of the program. Policies also will have to be developed regarding the storage and care of equipment, duties of custodians, the kind of inventory, who makes it and when, how equipment is to be marked and issued, the use of lockers, equipment, towels, etc.

It is well to remember that since most students take part in recreation just to have fun, it is important that their recreation be enjoyable. While the students are having a good time, however, the recreation administration must do everything possible to enrich their lives. Policies established for every aspect of the program should be in harmony with the underlying purpose: to insure the fulfillment of human needs.

All policies should be put in writing. This prevents misunderstanding about the how, what, when, and where of the school recreation program.

Use of School Facilities

Each school should develop a manual for the use of its facilities. The manual should be self-explanatory, specific and thorough. If this is well done and the established policies adhered to this should aid in preventing the destruction of property, lessen the number of personal injuries and numerous questions. The manual should tell for what, by whom, and how the swimming pool, courts, playing fields, recreation rooms, craft materials, musical instruments and so on should be used. The type of shoes or other clothing to be worn by participants should also be designated.

The manual can serve many purposes. It should include a calendar of events for the school year, diagrams indicating the pattern of administration, who does what, and providing other pertinent information essential to the supervisors and the participants.

Budget Making

The destiny of a school recreation program is dependent upon adequate financing. Until recently, it has been the policy in education to support financially only curricular or academic activities. Now there is a growing trend toward using tax funds to pay for extracurricular activities. In many instances, however, schools are still forced to supplement their extracurricular activities' funds with money from gate receipts derived from varsity sports, student fees, entrance fees, the sale of programs, and profits from movies, plays, circuses, and other forms of entertainment.

If the director is dependent upon variable sources of income and is not permitted to have an established budget, the program often will fall below expectations. The director needs to know how much money can be spent each year for program development, and an annual pre-established budget is important.

The proposed budget should be based upon an equipment inventory and staff recommendations of what is needed. Proposed costs must be compared with the amount of money that may conceivably be available. The budget request should be based on an honest appraisal of what is needed, but it may be unrealistic or even detrimental to the program to request *everything* that is desired in a given year.

Once the budget is established, it is essential that the recreation director keep an accurate account of all income and expenditures. Lack of fiscal control usually spells doom for most programs. It is recommended that a ledger be developed so that each expenditure can be recorded in a businesslike manner.

Use of Volunteer Leadership

The salaried director is the only person who can be held responsible for the success or failure of the school recreation program. Since most school programs are very much understaffed, it is essential that the recreation director capitalize as much as possible on good volunteer leadership. In practically all instances, the director will have to recruit and then train the volunteers to help in all phases of the program. They may come from a large variety of sources.

First, the school faculty should be canvassed for teacher leadership. Often, these persons are not only willing but anxious to help with parts of the program. This is especially true if they are asked to assist with activities in which they already have an interest.

Second, the director should canvass the entire student body for students who have special talent in leadership and specific skills. After recruiting the student leaders, considerable time will have to be spent in giving them in-service training. If this is not done one can expect the students to go off in different directions with a minimum of resulting overall success.

In the elementary and secondary schools in particular, one of the great reservoirs for volunteer leaders is the local parent-teacher association. The students are their children, so parents can be motivated to give of their own special talents to the development of a dynamic recreation program.

The personnel of the character-building volunteer agencies have had special training in working with youth groups. These people are especially equipped to work with boys and girls up through the secondary schools. Some of the best known of these agencies throughout the United States are Girl Scouts, Boy Scouts, Camp Fire Girls, Young Men's Christian Association, Young Women's Christian Association, American Red Cross, American Athletic Union, 4-H Clubs, Boys Clubs of America, and Woodcraft Rangers. Personnel of these and many other similar organizations are only awaiting invitations to assist the schools with their recreation programs.

Emergency Procedures

The recreation leader must always be prepared to give emergency first aid. This means that recreation personnel must maintain active Red Cross first aid and lifesaving credentials. Laymen should never diagnose or treat any illness, but render emergency first aid only. The first aid kit should be completely supplied and available at all times.

In anticipation of problems in this area, it is recommended that the recreation office maintain a reference file on all students. These individual student file cards should give such essential information as the student's address, parents' or next-of-kin's telephone number, the doctor's telephone number, and any other items deemed necessary for emergency use.

The recreation director may often conduct activities after the rest of the regular school staff has gone home. For this reason, the telephone numbers of the police department, fire department, an available doctor, and other essential emergency aid numbers should be posted where available for instant use.

Interest Inventory

Even though the recreation director thinks he knows what kinds of activities the students desire, he should occasionally conduct questionnaire surveys or use other appropriate methods to make sure he is right. Making an interest inventory is also a good public relations device for promoting the leisure-time program. A form such as that shown in the appendix could be used for this purpose.

Evaluation

All parts of the school recreation program should be continuously evaluated. This can be done in several different ways. Frequently the evaluation will be subjective in nature, but this is not necessarily a drawback. Subjective evaluation performed by a qualified individual is about as good as any other form of measurement. The methods used most frequently are:

1. Observation — subjective and objective phases
2. Questionnaires — to participants, to experts, to the student body
3. Interest inventories
4. Appraisal forms
5. Rating scales
6. Interviews
7. Case studies
8. Inspection reports
9. Self-rating forms
10. Discussion groups
11. Evaluation by outside groups

The director of recreation should develop various appraisal forms as an aid in the evaluation of all parts of the recreation program. The evaluation forms shown in the appendix have been used very effectively in improving campus recreation programs.

STAFF ORGANIZATION

Most school recreation departments find it advisable to diagram the administrative staff structure. The charts shown on the following pages are presented as samples of organizational structures used by different schools throughout the United States.

THE RECREATION ASSOCIATION

A well organized recreation association is important. The association should develop a constitution and by-laws to govern its operations. It is not necessary to construct a long list of rules and regulations. What is needed is a clear indication of the purposes and procedures by which the association functions. The following constitution has been found adequate for a recreation association.

CONSTITUTION OF THE UNIVERSITY RECREATION ASSOCIATION

ARTICLE I
NAME

The name of this organization shall be the University Recreation Association of the University of ....

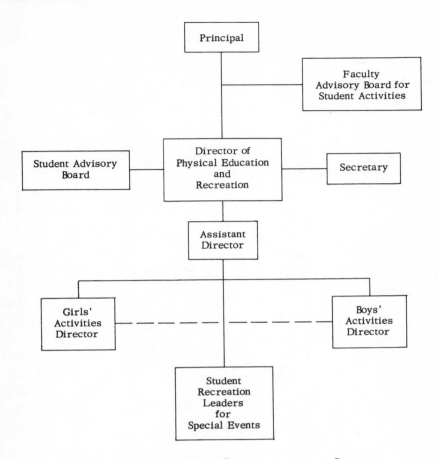

ORGANIZATION OF THE RECREATION IN A SMALL
ELEMENTARY, JUNIOR HIGH, OR SENIOR HIGH SCHOOL

Figure 6.1

ARTICLE II
PURPOSE

The purpose of this organization is to: 1) provide a permanent University Recreation Association; 2) initiate recreational activities and provide for the participation therein of all men and women of the University.

ARTICLE III
PARTICIPATION

All members of the Associated Students of the University of
.... and faculty members of the

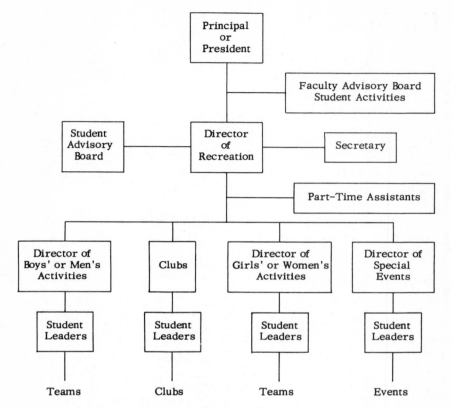

ORGANIZATION OF THE RECREATION PROGRAM IN
A SMALL COLLEGE OR LARGE HIGH SCHOOL

Figure 6.2

University of .... shall be privileged
to participate in the activities sponsored by this organization.

ARTICLE IV

ORGANIZATION

A. The activities of the organization shall be administered by the
University Recreation Board under the direction of the University
Recreation Association Executive Council.

1. The Executive Council shall be composed of: University Recreation
   Chairman, the Men's Intramural Chairman, the Women's Recreation
   Chairmen, one man and one woman faculty representative from the
   Physical Education Department.

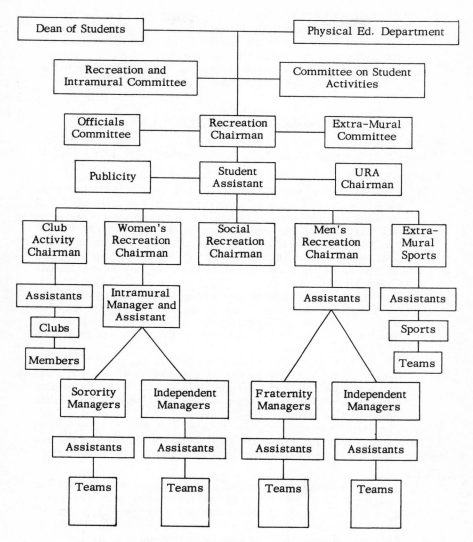

UNIVERSITY RECREATION ASSOCIATION-ORGANIZATION
(University of Southern California)

Figure 6.3

2. The University Recreation Board shall consist of: Executive Council, the Fraternity Athletic Managers, the Independent Sports Chairmen, and Chairman of each activity sponsored by the University Recreation Board.

B. Duties of the Executive Council
1. The Executive Council shall meet at the call of the University Recreation Chairman to discuss the business of the organization and make recommendations to the board.
2. The Executive Council shall initiate and coordinate all activities of the University Recreation Board.

ARTICLE V
APPOINTMENTS AND ELECTIONS

A. All appointments to the Executive Council and chairmen of the seasonal activities shall be made by the University Recreation Board.

B. Appointments:
1. University Recreation Chairman — Any student who has completed sixty (60) units of university work and who has a 2.5 cumulative grade average with a 2.0 in the preceding semester, who has received the recommendation of the University Recreation Board, shall be eligible for appointment to this office by the newly elected president of the A.S.S.C. for the coming year, and shall be given a non-voting seat on the University Student Senate Committee.
2. The Independent Students Sports Chairman — Any student who has completed sixty (60) units of university work and who has a 2.5 cumulative grade average with a 2.0 in the preceding semester is eligible to be appointed by the University Recreation Board to this position.
3. The Co-recreational Sports Chairman — Any female student who has completed sixty (60) units of university work and who has a 2.5 cumulative grade average with a 2.0 in the preceding semester is eligible to be appointed by the University Recreation Board to this position.
4. The Inter-Fraternity Athletic Manager — A male student who is appointed by the Inter-Fraternity council is eligible for this position. He must meet the grade point requirements listed above.

C. Elections:
1. The Men's Intramural Chairman — Any male student who has completed sixty (60) units of university work and who has a 2.5 cumulative grade average and a 2.0 in the preceding semester who has received the official recommendation of the University Recreation Board, shall be eligible for appointment to this office by the male students of the university during the Associated Men Students' Elections.
2. The Women's Recreation Chairmen — Any female student who has completed sixty (60) units of university work and who has a cumulative grade point average of 2.5 and a 2.0 in the preceding semester, who has received the official recommendation of the University Recreation Board shall be eligible for appointment to this office.
3. Officers of all clubs are elected by the members of each club. Qualifications for a club sponsored by the URA include:

a. 15 member minimum
b. chairman-headed officer and a committee of three or more
c. faculty sponsor
d. written constitution
e. approval of URA Executive Board
f. proposed future program
g. proposed budget
h. meeting place, facilities, equipment provided for
i. representation at URA council meetings by club chairman and one club representative.

ARTICLE VI
BY-LAWS AND QUORUM

1. A two-thirds majority of the University Recreation Board shall be required for the adoption or amendment to the By-Laws.

2. Two-thirds of the completed membership of the University Recreation Executive Council shall constitute a quorum of that body

ARTICLE VII
AUTHORITY

The board shall operate under the chairmanship of the University Recreation Chairman, who in the past has been defined as the Director of Recreation.

Chapter 7

Motivation

Motivation refers to an inner drive or need which tends to cause a person to do something; it provides the power which results in specific action. The power may be generated either by external or internal stimuli. An understanding of human behavior, particularly motivation, is indispensable to all those concerned with school recreation: leaders, teachers, and parents.

DISTINCTION AMONG TERMS

Interests

When an individual is interested in something, he is curious about it; it demands his attention. Characteristically, he displays concern and intentness toward it. The range and depth of interest, however, may vary from one extreme to another. While a person's interests are limited to some degree by native ability, they are determined largely by training and environment. Uneducated, unskilled, undirected, indigent individuals seldom show broad or deep interests in many things.

Motives

This is a generalized term which refers to those things that direct or determine behavior. One may or may not be conscious of the motive that initiates a specific action. The basic motives are unlearned and depend upon physiological need, but other motives are acquired. It is important that recreation leaders understand how motives can be learned, realize the power of association and substitution, understand the motives that tend to stimulate sustained interest in wholesome recreational activities, and recognize the need for satisfying experiences.

Drives

Tension that induces activity is known as drive. There are primary and acquired drives. The primary drives include such physiologically based needs as hunger, sex, pain, and so on. These are direct urges, fundamental and elemental needs. The word drive, when used in this manner, is synonymous with instinct. It is of significance to note here that some psychologists include the drive for muscular activity in their lists of fundamental impelling forces.

Secondary drives refer to urges acquired through experience and education, such as likes and dislikes. Since most drives are the result of learning, the great contribution which leaders, teachers, and their associates can make becomes obvious, and their responsibilities in this regard become exceedingly clear.

Incentives

An incentive is something that is used to stimulate interest and alter behavior. Positive incentives, such as praise and reward, are effective in

motivating persons to participate in recreational activities. Participation itself, competition, and social status also are impelling motives. Perhaps the most popular rewards used as incentives in recreation are letters, sweaters, watches, medals, ribbons, trophies, certificates, and newspaper publicity. Some say that it is very unwise to place emphasis on this form of motivation. They believe that one should enter recreational activities for the sheer enjoyment of participation and not for some extrinsic reward. This seems plausible; however, it is doubtful if very much could be found wrong in giving token rewards or prizes. If nonmaterial awards can help to initiate action and participation in wholesome recreational activities, their use seems justifiable. It is to be hoped, of course, that the motive for participation will shift in time from the desire to win a ribbon to the desire for the benefits of the activity itself.

Purposes

This term refers to action directed toward a specific goal. When a person has a purpose it can be assumed that he is aware of a goal, has constructed a plan of action for its attainment, and is in the process of carrying out this plan. It is essential that a person has interest, a motive, a drive, a purpose, and an incentive in order to achieve maximum results.

There never has been greater need for purposeful motivation. Required are ideas that stir the imagination. Why are we living? What contributions can we make toward an improved society? What really are the most important things in life? How can we help others to get more out of living? Why do we need recreation? How can we stimulate sustained interest in wholesome leisure-time activities? If people can become excited about what they do during their leisure time, perhaps they will develop real interest in many worthwhile activities.

DEVELOPING INTEREST IN SCHOOL RECREATION

The following ideas have been found very successful in stimulating and maintaining student interest in school recreational activities:

1. Offer a well-diversified program, scheduling more than one activity at a given time. The broader the program, the more likely it is that each person will find an activity which interests him.
2. Provide ample and adequate facilities for each activity that is offered.
3. Schedule the same activities often enough so that interest can be sustained.
4. Encourage intersquad, interclass, homeroom, interclub, and interfraternity competition.
5. Offer some co-recreational activities.

6. Utilize varsity lettermen for coaches and trainers of interclass and intramural competition.
7. Encourage the champion intramural teams to play the champion intramural teams of other schools.
8. Encourage spectator attendance at all final games.
9. Develop specific eligibility rules that are enforceable. Make sure that all students understand all rules.
10. Attempt to get maximum school and community newspaper coverage.
11. Develop attractive and informative bulletin boards.
12. Utilize assembly programs to make essential announcements.
13. Encourage the election of class, fraternity, homeroom, and athletic representatives to keep up interest.
14. Suggest that the best intramural players try out for the varsity team.
15. Solicit the aid of established school leaders. Encourage and assist the "key" men and women in each organization to stimulate interest in recreation in their specific organizations.
16. Solicit the cooperation of all teachers in the promotion of school recreation.
17. Award appropriate certificates, numerals, letters, medals, shields, cups, banners, pennants, or trophies to winners.
18. Secure adequate coverage in the school annual.
19. Place pictures of various activities and winning teams on appropriate bulletin boards.
20. Develop a recreation handbook and make it available to all students. Include pictures and statistics of all recreational activities.
21. Use mimeographing service, postcards, and the telephone to stimulate interest and information about the school recreation program.
22. Keep records of all-time champions for all individual events.
23. Select a good student reporter for the school and community newspaper.
24. Encourage all those assisting in the promotion of school recreation to be alert and imaginative in stimulating interest and favorable attitudes toward the school recreation program.
25. Make every effort to have excellent officiating for all sports events.
26. Encourage the selection of all-star teams for each activity.
27. Insist on good sportsmanship and fair play in all activities.
28. Schedule intramural games as "preliminaries" to varsity games. Sometimes the final quarter of various recreational contests can be played during half-times of varsity contests.
29. Schedule appropriate practice periods for all teams.
30. Insist on impartial and efficient management and supervision.
31. Never overlook the minutest details relating to all phases of organization and administration.

32. Organize a faculty advisory committee.
33. Encourage faculty participation in recreational activities.
34. Explore the possibility of offering academic credit to regular participants. This is an accepted practice in some schools for those who make debate teams, school bands, school chorus groups, and for those who are active in drama.
35. Encourage appropriate parties, picnics, and banquets in an effort to develop better understanding of the recreation offerings among the students.
36. Secure the cooperation of all school health services for the protection of students taking part in the school recreation program.

THE SCHOOL'S RESPONSIBILITY

The board of education, the superintendent, the principal, all teachers, the parent-teachers association, and the community in general are responsible for the welfare and happiness of the student body. It is high time that they collectively reassess all educational objectives in light of the unprecedented combination of forces that are currently reshaping our basic patterns of life. Since a great portion of man's life is spent in leisure, educators must attempt to abolish recreational illiteracy. The cultivation of talents and development of leisure-time skills are essential to cultural maturity.

Chapter 8

Legal Aspects of School Recreation

Can the public schools legally promote, organize, and conduct school recreational programs? If so, what are the legal responsibilities of recreational personnel relating to objectives, organization, finance, administration, control, liability, negligence, torts, nuisances, and moral obligations?

Legislation pertaining to school recreation cannot be separated entirely from the laws applicable to education in general. The legal aspects of school recreation can best be understood, therefore, by first examining the development of the educational system in this country. Each stage of progress has been marked by legislative actions designed to expand, restrict, control, or in some way direct the formal schooling of youth.

BACKGROUND FOR LEGAL ACTION

Early Educational Theory

The colonists believed human life to be amenable to great improvement. They also held strongly to the principle that man inherits certain natural rights including security of life, person, and property; the privilege of pursuing personal happiness; and the exercise of liberty or self-direction. Colonial leaders seem to have agreed that education was the principal means through which government could improve life and assure the welfare and happiness of the people.

COLONIAL EDUCATION. In general, when the early colonists came to the new world they set up the kinds of schools they had known in Europe but with specific adaptations to fit the new environment. Establishment of town schools was accomplished by vote at town meetings, and as early as 1636 the Massachusetts Colony agreed to contribute to the founding of Harvard College. In 1642, laws were passed to assure that children were taught to read. In 1647, every town of over fifty families was required to establish an *Elementary School,* and every town of 100 families had to provide a *Latin Grammar School,* where major emphasis was placed on reading and writing in Latin. In addition to these schools, the early colonists formed numerous *Private, Dame, Kitchen,* and *Religious schools.*

During the 1700's there was a growing belief that children needed more practical education than was offered by the *Elementary* or *Latin*

Grammar Schools. For this reason, Benjamin Franklin led a movement to establish a new type of school, the *Academy.* The curriculum of the *Academy* emphasized preparation for jobs in business, trade, navigation, surveying, and so forth. In time, the *Academy* became more popular than the *Latin Grammar School.*

LEGAL BASIS FOR EDUCATION

No direct reference to education can be found in the Constitution of the United States. The First and Tenth Amendments are significant however and, in fact, form the legal basis of public education. The First Amendment states:

> Congress shall make no law respecting an establishment of religion or prohibiting the free exercise thereof; or abridging the freedom of speech or of the press. . .

The Tenth Amendment declares:

> The powers not delegated to the United States by the Constitution, or prohibited by it to the States, are reserved to the States respectively, or to the people.

Through interpretation of these Constitutional amendments, education has been recognized from the beginning as a function of the state. Schools exist as state institutions because the very existence of civil society demands them. The state legislature therefore has plenary power in determining educational policy, qualifications of teachers, and the curricula of all public schools within the state.

States find it necessary when providing and controlling education to exercise what is known as "police power." Generally speaking, this power is inherent in a state's responsibilities in securing and promoting the general welfare of the citizens in the state. This "police power" implies that it is a state's duty to assure the comfort and convenience, public peace, public health, public morals, and public safety of its citizens. One can readily see that this power embraces almost every law concerned with the welfare of the citizens of each state.

Parts of the power may be delegated to agencies such as school districts, which are quasi-corporations created for the purposes of state administration. The courts seem to be in agreement that school districts are permitted the following privileges: (1) powers expressly granted by statute; (2) powers that are implied in those granted by statute; (3) powers that are essential to the accomplishment of objectives of the school district.

It is well established that school districts have the authority to maintain public education, including junior colleges; to require physical examinations of the pupils; to employ nurses, dentists, and physicians for inspectoral and diagnostic purposes; to maintain clinics; to provide for student teaching; to employ legal counsel; and to insure school property and teachers. The school districts may also build and maintain gymnasiums, swimming pools, playgrounds, and other kinds of recreational facilities when they promote the cause of education, better the schools, or keep the pupils and teachers contented.

Although control of the public schools resides with state and local government, the legislative branch of the federal government from time to time has concerned itself with education. For example, as early as 1787 Congress passed the *Northwest Ordinance*. This provided that education was to be forever encouraged in new states to be formed from territory then in the national domain. In 1862 the Morrill Act made it possible and legal for federal land to be used for the support of state agricultural and mechanical colleges. In 1874 the Kalamazoo Case made it legal to levy taxes for the support of public high schools, elementary schools, and state universities.

In recent years the federal government has increased its interest in education by passing laws such as the Serviceman's Readjustment Act of 1944 and, in 1958, the National Defense Education Act.

LEGAL BASIS FOR SCHOOL RECREATION

The schools in most states have a long history of recreational services rendered to the community. The authorization for these has generally been cloaked under several legal provisions:

Civic Center Laws. Most states have enacted laws permitting use of school facilities by the community when they are not being used by the school.

Community Recreation Enabling Laws. Most states have enacted legislation which makes it permissible to levy taxes for the support of recreational programs that contribute to the attainment of general education and worthy use of leisure time.

Enabling acts are laws which permit managing authorities to establish, organize, administer, and conduct recreation programs. Enabling legislation should include several broad provisions such as naming the managing authority; permitting joint exercise of powers act (combined school and community forces); employment of qualified personnel; authority to refuse and buy property; power to vote bonds; power to levy taxes; power to acquire and use properties outside the school district, and power to equip, operate, and maintain recreational areas and facilities.

The education code, a publication of the state board of education, usually specifies the legal extent to which schools can conduct recreation programs. In most cases there is considerable latitude, allowing the operation of extracurricular programs.

Information About Legal Authority

Recreation personnel should acquaint themselves with all legislation relating to the development of school recreation in their specific school and state and to the authority granted recreation administrators. The basic sources are the state laws, education code, rules and regulations prescribed by the state board of education, opinions of the attorney general, and decisions of the court. Other sources that could be invaluable are the harbors and navigation code, health and safety code, military and veterans code, public resources code, street and highways code, vehicle code, and the welfare institutions code. All of these codes have implications that are important to the recreational director.

LEGAL LIABILITY

The disposition of legal matters varies widely throughout the United States. Very little legal structure can be outlined that would be applicable to all the states. The following interpretations, however, are fairly accurate in most situations.

Pupil Control. When parents send their children to school, they delegate to the teacher authority to discipline them for offenses committed against the proper order and effective operation of the school. This power given by the parent (in *loco parentis*) must be used reasonably. Punishment must be warranted, be administered without malice, and not be so severe that the student receives permanent harm. In other words, whatever the teacher does must be justified and performed in good faith.

In general, the school may temporarily suspend a student. School boards have the right to expel a student permanently when he refuses to obey some reasonable rule. On occasions, even when no rule exists, if the pupil's conduct is detrimental to the interest of the school, he may be expelled.

Negligence. Teachers and school recreation leaders are personally liable for their own negligence. Often the courts refer to negligence in the following manner: *nonfeasance* — failure to perform an act at all; *misfeasance* — failure to perform an act properly. If they have unreasonably *failed* to anticipate danger, to adhere to a proper standard of conduct, to administer first aid, or to act, in general, in a prudent manner, they can be found guilty of negligence.

Court findings have indicated that the most common sources of negligence include use of defective equipment; failure to use mats in gymnastic classes or proper padding around obstructions in the gymnasium and on the playfield; permitting ill or injured students to participate in activities; teaching activities that are not a part of the prescribed program; forcing students to attempt movements that they fear, and allowing students to take part in activities without proper instruction in safety procedures.

In the past, most legal suits charging negligence have been based on physical injury to the student. Lately, certain injuries that fall outside the field of physical disability have been grounds for suits.

Informed parents are rightfully demanding that their children receive maximum protection from obvious social and mental influences that are corrosive in nature and are occasionally associated with poorly supervised recreation programs. Immature minds are sometimes faced with disquieting frustrations and hypnotic impulses. These emotional experiences, if undirected, can lead to unacceptable habit patterns. Adequately trained recreation leaders know how to avoid, eliminate, alter, or counteract most of the causative influences.

Judicial bodies are aware of our educational responsibilities. They are also cognizant of what can be accomplished by qualified teachers and recreational leaders. With the knowledge that our profession now possesses, the unproductive educator may be legally charged with *demonstrative negligence*. Tests can be devised that would measure to a significant degree the effectiveness of every teacher and recreation leader. In other words, we may be negligent if we fail to produce.

SPECIFIC ACTS OF NEGLIGENCE

Court decisions, together with numerous recorded judicial opinions, have emphasized certain responsibilities in the organization, supervision, and administration of school recreational programs. Some of those responsibilities in which negligence may be charged follow.

1. If the recreation director authorizes a student to participate in a strenuous recreational activity without previously having had a physical examination, and if an injury occurs due to some disability that the examination might have revealed.

2. When a student is permitted to enter an organized strenuous activity without first having gone through a physical conditioning process, and if an injury occurs because he was not in good physical condition.

3. When a student is permitted to participate in an organized activity in which he was injured that is beyond his performance level and in which he had not learned sufficient skills and knowledges to reasonably protect himself from a physical injury.

4. When a student injures himself in an organized activity in which the director has failed to stress safety and has also failed to use adequate safety devices such as mats, eyeglass guards, human spotters, lifeguards, and so forth.

5. When a student injures himself in an organized activity and the supervisor fails to use appropriate first aid techniques and this results in further injury.

6. When an activity is taught and the students are encouraged to take unreasonable risks, and an injury occurs due to these risks.

7. In an organized activity conducted in a location where the conditions are considered to be unsafe, and if an injury occurs due to unsafe conditions.

8. When a student is permitted to take part in an organized recreational activity in which he has not been acquainted with the dangerous aspects of this activity, and if an injury occurs due to his lack of this specific information.

9. When a student is injured in a school recreational program and the injury was due to unauthorized transportation by school personnel.

10. When a student is injured in an organized school recreational activity due to any of the following causes: inadequate numbr of supervisors; lack of facility controls; lack of proper rules and regulations to assure safe usage; absence of faculty supervision; poor judgment on the part of the supervisor; absence of reasonable foresight by the supervisor; improper classification of students for participation; play area too congested; lack of extra precautions during peak load hours; failure to utilize a progressive sequence of activities; inadequate supervisorial personnel; inadequate separation of students with reference to size, age, maturity, and sex; and lack of planned emergency procedures.

Contributory Negligence

If the injured person's behavior or conduct indicates that he failed to act as a reasonably prudent student should have under the circumstances, and if his actions contributed to the accident, negligence on the part of the teacher or leader is discounted.

Assumption of Risk

The courts recognize the inherent danger in all physical activities. The participant therefore assumes certain risks when he takes part in active recreation. There thus is no liability for injury unless negligence can be proven. The teacher or recreation leader would not be found liable for an injury if he could prove that he had properly taught the skill in question, had acquainted the student with adequate safety measures, and had taught the student as a reasonably prudent instructor would have under the circumstances. Since there is an *assumption* of risk on the part of the participants, the teachers and recreation leaders are liable only when their action falls below an accepted standard for the situation.

Moral Responsibility

Recreation leaders are morally obligated to the maximum of their ability to motivate, teach, and protect all students.

Attractive Nuisance

Young people generally are attracted to swimming pools, gymnasiums, and playfields. These frequently present hazardous situations, facilities and equipment that may endanger life or seriously impair health. Although schools and communities have established various controls over such areas to prevent accidents, it is well known that many dangers still exist. The courts have held school districts responsible for injuries attributed to unsupervised hazardous areas and have repeatedly granted compensation for injuries attributed to legally identified attractive nuisances.

LIABILITY INSURANCE

It is recommended that all recreational personnel carry extensive individual liability insurance. Where possible, all students should be protected by accident insurance. Several major insurance companies have special low-rate policies that will cover most recreational accidents.

REPORTS AND WAIVERS

Accident Report

A complete report should be made out for each accident that occurs in the school recreation program. This report should include a full description of how the accident occurred, all extenuating circumstances, and what was done after the accident occurred; information should be given such as first aid rendered, doctor summoned, and so on. This report should be signed by at least three witnesses plus the supervisor in charge of the specific activity in which the accident occurred.

Waivers

Signed permission slips by either parents or students have little value in protecting the recreation director from a lability suit. Parents cannot sign away the legal rights of minors.

JUDICIAL CHANGES

During the past few years thinking concerning the school's liability for torts, negligence, and other acts or omissions committed by the teacher seems to be undergoing marked changes. Legal action is usually established by previous court decisions. Since school recreation is a rather new endeavor, few precedents exist. Judging by present trends, one can logically assume that new patterns of responsibility are likely to arise in this profession in the near future.

Chapter 9

History and Values of Intramural Sports

Intramural sports activities frequently are considered the most essential part of the school recreational program. Certainly they contribute to the physical, social, mental, and moral development of the entire student body.

The term *intramural* is derived from the Latin words *intra*, meaning within, and *muralis*, meaning wall; it therefore means the activities connected within the walls of a school. This term probably dates back to the "city-state" days in ancient Greece, when most cities were encircled by walls.

DEVELOPMENT OF INTRAMURAL SPORTS

Competitive athletics were practically nonexistent in the United States during the Colonial period. The people were so busily occupied solving everyday problems that very little free time existed. The rigors of living, coupled with the belief that it was not wise, righteous, or profitable to waste time in such play activities, precluded the possibility of much interest in sports (62:145). During Colonial times, no time was given to play or recreation in the school program. Midway through the eighteenth century, however, school authorities began to give some recognition to the values and importance of physical exercise. It was at this time that the academies developed a broader and more comprehensive view of the school program (58:477).

The rise of military academies, early in the nineteenth century, gave another stimulus to interest in physical education, military drill, and other

forms of physical exercise. At about this time also an intense, flaming na-
·tionalist spirit burst into full flame, causing Congress to authorize the
creation of a national army and navy. This action in turn encouraged participation in physical activity for the development and maintenance of
physical fitness.

Prior to the Civil War, organized physical recreation consisted almost
entirely of aquatics and gymnastics; the earliest physical recreation in the
American schools very definitely reflected this European interest. Indeed,

we borrowed many European ideas about sports and sport clubs. During
and immediately following the Civil War, the Turnverein became prominent; this organization initiated numerous competitions and prizes and
awards were given the winners of gymnastic contests.

Shortly after the beginning of the twentieth century several colleges
and universities established intramural sports programs, and numerous
high schools quickly followed this precedent. At the present time, the
practice is widespread throughout the nation. Intramurals are an established and respected form of sports competition, enthusiastically supported by participants and administrators. It is unfortunate that there are
still many schools that have failed to organize intramurals for their students.

PURPOSES OF INTRAMURAL SPORTS

The aim of intramural sports is to provide appropriate competitive physical activities for the students within a given school. The activities should be adapted to the facilities, needs, interests, abilities, and maturity of the students. If this is done, it is strongly believed that immediate and long-term values will accrue from the sports program. Some of the most apparent contributions of a school intramural program follow.

Social Growth

Barring a world-wide catastrophe, people will continue to migrate toward urban habitations. This bunching process makes it more essential that we have a greater understanding than formerly of our fellow man. We need to learn more about each other's likes, dislikes, whims and peculiarities. We must develop helpfulness, friendliness, trustworthiness, and loyalty. We need to understand the importance of cooperation and teamwork because it has become difficult in today's world to pull oneself up alone by his own bootstraps.

It is easy to see by following this line of thought that one purpose of the intramural program is to serve as a social laboratory, a place where one can observe, learn to evaluate and to analyze the attributes approved by society. The more society tends to cluster, the more important this objective becomes.

Through play one learns to estimate an individual's abilities, his weaknesses, his assets, his character, and his personality (57:272,ff), for when a person plays he has a tendency to lower his guard. Many of his true characteristics are exposed to the observing mind and eye. If we have been taught the true values of life by our parents, teachers, and leaders, we should be able to evaluate the actions of those with whom we play. This should help us in selecting those whom we would like for companions and in improving society.

Intramurals afford a wonderful opportunity to practice well-bred behavior through friendly contests. At the same time, we are able to arouse intergroup interest and develop group and school loyalty. Furthermore, intramurals afford excellent opportunities to break down long-established barriers stemming from different colors, creeds, religions, and beliefs. If we are to live in the same community and go to the same schools, then we must try to understand each other. This is essential to the democratic way of life.

Worthy Use of Leisure Time

A portion of everyone's leisure time should be spent in wholesome physical recreation. This is extremely important during adolescence. Intramurals provide maximum opportunities for students to experience the thrills of success, the humbleness in failure and the satisfactions of making their best efforts. Through these efforts students recognize when they have gone "all-out" in trying to achieve an objective. The satisfaction gained through self-expression and through the release of pent-up emotions ranks high as an intramural objective.

Wholesome recreation can relieve many ills. It sometimes lessens the emotional disturbance brought about by rejection, domineering parents, projection of parental ambition, unhappy family relationships, prejudices, and adjustments. It very definitely assists in lessening tension arising from socioeconomic differences in a given student body. It matters not so much who you are, but how you play the game.

If one of the major aims of education is the worthy use of leisure time, this certainly implies the need to promote civic responsibility. The leisure time activities sponsored by the schools should be conducted as an integral part of the total education process. We should strive to develop physically, mentally, emotionally, and socially fit citizens. This definitely suggests the need for a wide variety of activities in which many learnings take place at the same time.

If during a person's leisure time he could develop skills, attitudes, strength, endurance, self-realization, self-discovery, make social adjustments, improve his citizenship, enrich life's experiences, and increase cultural understanding about the world in which he lives, then this without doubt would be considered a worthy use of leisure time. If through play one improves physical well-being, develops good mental health, increases safety knowledge, and develops character, then again his leisure time has been employed in a worthy manner. Intramurals surely measure up in every respect as a commendable recreational pursuit.

Development of Physical Fitness

Many believe that urban life will become the Achilles heel of Western civilization. It is argued that we are bombarded with stimuli which tend to make each succeeding generation more inactive; in time, inertia will sap the great driving force inherited from our ancestors. For the sake of health, family, community, and nation, it is essential that the inclination toward inactivity be overcome and that we succeed in maintaining a state of adequate physical fitness. (57:219,f)

Physical fitness implies good muscular strength, coordination, agility, ability for sustained muscular activity, and resistance to organic disease. Good health, although a more inclusive term, is a condition that flows in part from wholesome living and physical fitness.

A state of physical fitness is usually achieved through exercises that emphasize walking, running, jumping, swimming, climbing, lifting, pushing, pulling throwing, and striking. Such actions are, of course, the very components of intramural sports. Intramurals thus provide opportunities for all students to participate in the wholesome, vigorous activities through which total body development is acquired with the greatest enthusiasm.

Prevention of Delinquency

When an offense is committed against the social order subscribed to by a given society, it is considered a delinquent act. When these forms of misconduct deviate sufficiently to warrant being considered a menace to oneself, to one's future interests or to society in general, this is called delinquency. There are no single rule-of-thumb methods or measures by which the predelinquent can be identified, nor should delinquency be regarded as a twenty-four hour a day malady. Nevertheless, when there are persisting signs of serious violations of the norms, delinquency generally follows.

Teachers can sometimes arrest tendencies toward delinquency through special guidance and counseling of students. Often the predelinquent is not aware that he is drifting toward a dangerous whirlpool or current that will take him off his basic course. A good understanding of the problem student's subculture makes it easier to determine which remedial techniques will be most effective in rehabilitation.

The physical education teacher and the recreation director probably have greater influence on more children than any other individual. It is helpful if these people can identify potential delinquents and select appropriate measures to counteract unfavorable influences and tendencies.

Intramural sports are one of the foes of delinquency. It has been said that it is more fun to hit a ball than to hit a person, that it is a greater thrill to steal a base than it is to steal an apple from a supermarket. Boys and girls wish to be active. Unless we provide desirable activities for them, they may find undesirable pastimes of their own. Interest in intramural sports can help to curb delinquency.

Other Values

It is not the primary aim of intramurals to act as a "feeder" for interscholastic athletics. Nevertheless, many varsity players are recruited from the ranks of intramural contestants. Successful experience develops additional interest in an activity; the interest so engendered sometimes spurs players to achieve higher levels of skill. Consequently, it can be expected that an occasional intramural player may make a varsity team.

School intramurals can be one of the best leadership training laboratories in the school, as there are countless opportunities for developing and exercising such ability in every phase of the program. Where else can students gain more experience in working with people, making decisions, planning, organizing and supervising, learning to promote and evaluate?

Finally, and perhaps most importantly, through intramural competition skills and interests in physical activity that can last a lifetime may be developed.

Chapter 10

Organization of the Intramural Program

There are different plans of organization for intramural sports. The complexity of the structure usually depends on the size of the school and the status of the program. The five most commonly used types of organization are (1) student controlled but under the supervision of a faculty member, (2) responsibility for promotion and control delegated to a teacher, (3) program conducted by the varsity coaches, (4) responsibility assumed by an intramural director with the help of student managers, (5) student controlled in every respect.

LEADERSHIP

Intramural programs that are organized, supervised, and administered completely by faculty members seldom afford students the opportunity for many leadership experiences. On the other hand, programs administered solely by students often lack definiteness of function and stability of organization. The best programs appear to have a proper combination of student and faculty planning.

It is difficult to state categorically whether a high school needs a full-time or a part-time director of intramural sports. The size of the school, the facilities available, and the content of the program will determine to a large extent the personnel required. In most high schools, the director has class teaching as a part of his work load.

A full-time director of intramural sports is employed by most of the larger universities. The development of a good program requires so great an expenditure of time and energy that it should be a full-time job. A

teacher who has to coach or teach other activities is unable to give sufficient attention to intramurals. Regardless of the fact that intramural
sports have been promoted successfully under different schemes of administration, the best arrangement is to have a full-time director, responsible for promoting and coordinating the various phases of the work.

This type of program is called the "centralized plan of organization."
The following assistants to the intramural director are examples of the
leadership positions that are helpful in the promotion and operation of
the program (56:27).

Assistant Director

If the intramural program is very large, an assistant director will be
invaluable. In general, he relieves the director of many of the details of
organization. He often is assigned the supervision of the student managers.

Field Supervisors

Field supervisors are needed when several games are taking place
at the same time. The supervisors make sure that the teams are at their
respective places; that referees, scorekeepers, and timers are available; that

scores are properly tabulated and turned in; and that all equipment is available.

Intramural Trainer

The intramural trainer is found only in larger schools. His responsibilities include the supervision of training for certain sports that require more than the usual amount of conditioning, endurance, and strength. He also gives special attention to the students who are in poor physical condition and renders first aid to the injured.

Intramural Student Manager

The intramural student manager heads a corps of student assistants. Because his position involves a great deal of work, some schools have two or three divisional managers during the school year. The major duties of the student manager are to assign assistants their work, to make out schedules, to assemble data from the contests, to prepare materials for the bulletin boards, and to act as a medium between the intramural office and the student body. Sometimes the manager acts as a field supervisor.

The intramural student manager usually is selected in one of two ways. He may be appointed by a committee composed of the intramural director, the assistant director, and the outgoing student manager, or he may be selected by popular vote of the students. The latter system is used frequently but often results in the selection of unqualified candidates.

Sports Managers

Sophomore staff members who have shown proficiency in their assignments usually are the ones selected to become sports managers during their junior year. It is customary to have a sport manager for each of the major sports. He is in charge of one specific activity.

Team Managers

Team managers are the representatives from each unit participating in the competition. They are the liaison persons between the intramural office and their respective teams. They receive and pass on to their teams all announcements pertaining to schedules, contests, rules, and so on.

Officials for Contests

Students with varsity athletic experience often make good officials of intramural contests. Their experience and prestige tend to make their decisions acceptable. Students majoring in physical education or recreation, staff members, and alumni who formerly were players often make good officials also.

Officiating practice is a valuable leadership experience, and it is strongly recommended that many students be given opportunity to conduct games. Faculty members often are glad to aid the program by officiating for it helps them to understand the students better.

Some schools pay small fees to the officials. This usually ranges between fifty cents to five dollars per game.

Committees

Some schools have intramural committees, such as the student committee — makes recommendations and voices complaints; faculty advisory committee — assists in developing policies; finance committee — assists in securing appropriate finances; awards committee; protest committee; and training committee.

Faculty Assistants

Faculty members should be assigned to assist the intramural director in administering the various activities. The value of the program is enhanced when there are as many faculty assistants as there are activities in progress at a given time. A rotating assignment schedule can be followed so that no one faculty member is constantly involved in the program.

Voluntary Student Leadership

Clubs, classes, and homerooms are commonly used as sources for student assistants. The number of assistants needed depends, of course, on the size of the school and its intramural program. It is advisable to have many helpers in the lower classes so that there will be a good selection of applicants for the more responsible leadership positions held by upperclassmen.

A leaders' club may well be the backbone of the intramural program in elementary and secondary schools. Such groups meet regularly during the activities period or after school and may serve as the governing body or executive board of the intramural program. The duties of the boys' leaders club at some high schools include numerous types of responsibilities that can be handled by a student group. The members appoint the presidents for each league, arrange schedules, promote new activities, and in general relieve the instructor of nearly all details in connection with the program. The leaders' club group in one instance were all members of various sport clubs and so provided liaison between the respective clubs and the governing body. The membership of the club was open to all boys, but they had to take an active part in the work of the club or be dropped from the roll (60:30).

Another plan for organizing the intramural program is to form an intramural athletic association to which every student in school belongs. The executive board of the association might consist of two representatives from each room who, as a group elect officers, or officers and executive board members might be elected by the total student body. The physical education instructor or recreation director acts as supervisor of all activities but does as little clerical and organizational work as possible.

Sometimes upper classmen known to have sufficient leadership qualities and knowledge of sports are recruited to take over a large share of the responsibility for intramural sports. Time must be spent with these leaders to train them for their duties, to exchange ideas, and to plan for the proposed events. At some schools, an athletic manager is either elected or appointed for each class. Each manager appoints a leader from each class who is responsible for helping promote student interest in games, tournaments, and special meetings or practices. The manager of each club is in complete charge, and the various leaders are responsible to him.

FINANCING THE INTRAMURAL PROGRAM

Most authorities agree that the cost of intramural sports should be covered by general school funds or by appropriations listed in the physical education budget. The reasoning is that since intramurals are a laboratory phase of education, the financial support of a program that benefits so many students should be stable and assured.

Other less desirable methods of financing intramural sports are appropriations from varsity athletics, money collected from carnivals, exhibitions, plays, concessions, student entry fees, and ticket sales to special events. There are objections to these sources of revenue. If intramurals depend on funds from interscholastic athletics, an overemphasis of the interscholastic program often results. It is generally agreed that the payment of entry fees is not in accord with the general aim of intramural activity. This system is a last resort when there is no backing from other sources.

A variety of methods can be used in handling intramural finances. The high school principal may be in charge of these funds in small high schools and the general school treasurer may have the responsibility in larger high schools. In colleges and universities, money may be controlled by the director of physical education, the intramural director, the student athletic association, a faculty committee, a faculty-student committee, or a dean of student affairs. Whoever manages the financial aspect of the program must have proper authority. Student help on financial matters may be used only if adequately supervised. A strict account, kept up-to-date, must be maintained in a businesslike manner.

THE PROGRAM

The intramural sports program should be based on the physical education curriculum and, in general, should follow the progression of seasonal instruction in all activities taught. Many individual and dual sports are, of course, participated in throughout the year, and competitions may be scheduled at any season. The intramural program may also enrich the physical education program by providing opportunities to participate in activities in which there is no formal instruction.

The types of activities should represent a balance between competitive team and individual-dual sports and noncompetitive recreational activities. Flexibility and variety in the program help in meeting the ever-changing interests and desires of the participants and the needs of everyone, from the very active to the restricted student. It is desirable that a number of activities be presented at the same time.

A list of activities may serve to suggest how the activities can be arranged into three seasons, fall, winter, and spring.

Activities by Season

Fall	Winter	Spring
Archery	Badminton	Archery
Cross-country running	Basketball	Baseball
Fencing	Bowling	Boating
Field hockey	Boxing	Canoeing
Football (flag-touch)	Free-throwing in	Diving
Golf	basketball	Golf
Hiking	Gymnastics	Gymnastics
Lacrosse	Handball	Hiking
Recreational games	Rhythms, dance	Horseshoes
Riding	Squash	Life saving
Riflery	Swimming	Roller skating
Soccer	Table tennis	Sailing
Speedball	Volleyball	Softball
Swimming	Water polo	Swimming
Tennis	Weight training	Tennis
Weight training	Wrestling	Track and field
		Volleyball

The climate and customs of a particular locality, and the availability of facilities, govern the choice of time for offering an activity. The chart on page 75 shows the schedule in effect in 1963 at a high school in Tennessee.

To a large extent, activities selected for the program will be determined by the training of the instructors and student helpers. Untrained
or poorly trained instructors and student helpers cannot administer and
conduct an efficient or successful intramural program; under any circumstances a program so conducted must be a very limited one.

High School Sports Calendar — 1963

Sports	Tournament or Event	Entries	Play Begins
Tennis (Doubles)	Elimination Tournament	Sept. 15 - 18	Sept. 19
Softball	Round Robin Tournament	Sept. 15 - 18	Sept. 20
Touch Football	Round Robin Tournament	Oct. 8 - 10	Oct. 11
Table Tennis	Elimination Tournament	Oct. 9 - 10	Oct. 13
Badminton	Double Elimination Tournament	Nov. 5 - 7	Nov. 8
Handball	Ladder Tournament	Nov. 5 - 7	Nov. 8
Basketball	Round Robin Tournament	Dec. 1 - 3	Dec. 5
Play Night	Coeducational Sports Program	Dec. 9 - 11	Dec. 12
Boxing	Elimination Tournament	Jan. 6 - 9	Jan. 10
Wrestling	Elimination Tournament	Feb. 2 - 6	Feb. 7
Volleyball	Ladder Tournament	Feb. 24 - 26	Feb. 27
Open House	Finals in Table Tennis, Badminton, Handball, Basketball, Boxing, Wrestling, and Volleyball		March 20
Horseshoes	Elimination Tournament	March 24 - 26	March 27
Track and Field	Track and Field Meet	April 14 - 16	April 17
Tennis (Singles)	Elimination Tournament	April 20 - 23	April 24
Decathlon	Three-day Meet	May 1 - 4	May 5
Field Day	Finals for Horseshoes and Tennis (Singles), last day of Decathlon, Softball games for all		May 8

The type of activities included in former programs also may influence
the selection of activities. If certain events have been customary for years,

it is difficult to eliminate them even if others have more value. This can be accomplished eventually by making changes gradually and slowly.

Intramural programs should stress outdoor activities whenever possible. In limited areas of the United States, outdoor programs can be conducted throughout the entire year; in other regions, the outdoor season is short.

Interest in specific activities depends upon the locale of the school, the age group, previous experiences of the participants, and leadership. The following activities seem however to be popular everywhere: basketball, baseball, softball, tennis, track and field, swimming, and golf. Basketball is undoubtedly the single most popular intramural activity in the United States.

SCHEDULING ACTIVITIES

Whenever possible, the intramural program should be conducted within or during an extension of the school day. Recess, class periods, noon-hour, and before and after school periods are the simplest time assignments for intramurals. At any of these times, however, conflicts in personnel and in the use of facilities are to be expected. It is well to consider the possibility of conducting the program during an activity period when the homeroom students are readily available. If the school day is lengthened so that an activity period occurs at the end, so much the better. Some schools have successfully scheduled their intramural programs at night, on week ends, in the mornings before school, and during vacation periods.

A definite time and place should be posted for each activity and the information should be circulated by the managers or team captains. If participants not available at the time of a contest, it is forfeited. Postponements are to be avoided when possible, for the program tends to lose its effectiveness if activities are allowed to drag on for long periods of time.

Facilities should be made available for use as they are needed. This involves not only time for tournament play but also opportunity for practices, training for activities, and playing on an informal basis.

SPECIAL CONSIDERATIONS

Medical Examinations

Physical examinations usually are required for competitors in interscholastic sports. This is especially true for strenuous activities such as basketball, track and field, boxing, wrestling, tennis, siwmming, and touch football. Students participating in the intramural program often will not be in as good a physical condition as those participating in the interscholastic sports. Inasmuch as one of the objectives of the intramural program is to promote health and safety, it should be a prime duty of leaders to insure protection for intramural athletes by requiring them to pass a physical examination successfully before participating in the more vigorous events.

Protests

Protests in competitive sports are to be avoided whenever possible. Protests should be permitted only on points that concern the interpretation of the rules of the game, the eligibility of a player, etc. Never should a case of appeal be allowed which involved mistakes of judgment by the officials. A decision such as whether a pitch was a ball or a strike, though it may have been incorrect, cannot be changed without entirely destroying the official's authority over the game (56:234).

Legitimate protests are those made in writing within twenty-four hours after the contest (72:280).

Forfeits

Forfeits are one of the largest sources of irritation for an intramural director, and the regulations governing them must be definite and clearly understood. The usual rule is that both teams shall be on the playing grounds ready for the game within ten minutes of the time assigned, or the game is awarded to the team present. If a very rigid time schedule is necessary because many games are being played, it may be necessary to reduce the time limit to five minutes. There are cases where neither organization has a full team present, but both teams appear later. Since both squads are at fault, it might be permissible to play a shortened game, if it is at least one-half as long as the regulation playing time. In the event of shortages in the line-up, the general rule is that a complete line-up must be present for two-man teams; for teams of from three to nine, not more than one may be missing; for teams requiring nine or more participants, not more than two may be absent.

If students and organizations regard their intramural participation as a privilege, there will be fewer forfeits. Forfeits may be reduced by placing a heavy penalty on them, such as the loss of points or privileges for the entire year. The latter, however, appears to be too severe in most cases, and tends in the long run to reduce the participation so desirable for all students.

Postponements

Postponements are one of the inevitabilities that must be accepted in intramural sports programs. The factor of postponement should be foreseen and provided for in the time schedule. On days of varsity games and large school functions, the intramural program probably should be omitted.

Following a postponement, arrangements must be made to play off the game at another time. In an elimination series, the games may simply be postponed for a day. In a league series where the schedule is made out in advance to cover the whole season the preceding method is impossible, since games are already set for the following round. The scheduled game must be played as arranged and the postponed game must remain undecided until there is an open date.

Chapter 11

Organization of the Extramural Program

The word *extramural* means "outside the walls," hence technically competition of any sort between schools is extramural competition.

Extramurals, as the term is usually used however, exclude highly organized, formally-scheduled varsity competition in athletics but refer rather to other kinds of competitive units from one school participating with similar units from other schools. Though coaches, particularly in junior or senior high school are sometimes given a school recreation assignment in addition to their varsity coaching duties, this practice is not recommended because almost inevitably the varsity assignment takes precedence. This is not to imply that competitive athletics at the varsity level cannot be recreational in nature, but unfortunately this is not always the case. Since ample material exists on the conduct of varsity athletics and since persons charged with this responsibility would not refer to recreational sources for help, a consideration of varsity athletics has been excluded from these pages.

EXTRAMURALS

Extramural sports have existed for many years to some extent. In many instances this program has afforded students their only opportunity to compete with others in sports. Typical examples can be found in numerous rural communities where schools are too scattered to warrant regularly organized competition. Extramurals offer the only competition in some schools, schools which are so small that intramural competition cannot be conducted. In large schools the practice is to take intramural champions, an all-star team from an intramural league, or merely teams made up of those who would like to compete, and play the same type of team from other like schools. Competition may be held in any sports activity.

Sometimes a number of schools located close to one another decide to organize an extramural association. They schedule their separate intramural activities so that every school concludes each activity at about the same time. Then the winning intramural team from each school takes part in an elimination tournament, perhaps for the city or county intramural championship. The constitution shown in the appendix was drawn up by a number of southern California colleges so they would follow the same procedures and thus make possible a good extramural program.

PLAY DAYS

Play days were first organized by women's physical education departments and apparently at one time completely or at least largely satisfied the girls' desire for varsity competition. Play days have been particularly successful with junior and senior high school girls and have also been used with both girls and boys of elementary school age. Play day competition is arranged by bringing together students from several schools and intermixing them so that each team is composed of players from different schools. Throughout the program activities are organized so that individual schools lose their identity during competition. Competition is based on some arbitrarily chosen team division and not on the "school against school" basis, as is characteristic of most other forms of school competition. In play-day competition, many students participate, sometimes all the girls from a school, sometimes all the girls in a specific class, sometimes representatives from each class. They may be organized with participants from other schools into "color teams." Often the play day has a theme in which case teams are called by appropriate names. In general, play days for girls at the junior and senior high school level have been used in lieu of interschool competition. Play days are occasional affairs, not formally scheduled league competition.

Aims and Objectives

In general, the aims and objectives of play days are similar to those of other educational endeavors, that is they should contribute to the emotional, social, educational, recreational, and physical development of the participants. A unique aspect of play days and one of their strengths is that emphasis is placed on participation by many players and on a variety of activities. There is practically no spectator emphasis. Not only are a number of different activities played simultaneously, but the level of play is much more social and recreational than competitive. It is felt that play day experiences provide opportunity for participants to make new acquaintances, to learn to play together harmoniously, and for joy alone. Play days almost always end with some kind of social occasion and refreshments so participants learn how to be gracious hostesses and guests.

Program of Activities

Sometimes a play day is organized into two divisions of activities namely team sports, and individual and dual sports. The team sports division often consists of basketball, volleyball, field hockey, softball, and speed-a-way or speedball. The individual and dual sports section often includes swimming, track and field, table tennis, badminton, and archery. Generally the players are shifted from one court or field to another at about fifteen minute intervals so that opportunity is given for playing with many participants. More typically, the program of activities for a play day is chosen with reference to the theme of the day. Games and relays which are appropriate to the theme are preferred. Regardless of what is played, however, the teams are given names which are suitable to the occasion.

Themes, Programs, and Badges

The themes for play days generally are derived from seasons, holidays, cultures, history, sports, and many novelty ideas.

The printed programs should be attractive, carry out the theme, be informative, complete and small enough to fit in a shirt pocket.

Name tags should carry out the theme and provide space for the participant's name and school. They should not be so large as to interfere with freedom of movement while playing.

Finance

The financing of play days is generally an insignificant factor. The small expense incurred is usually secured from one or more of the following sources: student body funds, Girls Athletic Association, Girls League, or entrance fees from participants or participating schools. It is recommended that necessary funds be secured from the student body fund.

Refreshments and Entertainment

Usually at the end of a play day, the hostess school provides simple refreshments such as cookies and punch. Often at this same time special entertainment also is provided. This may include singing, music, dancing, skits and so on, again activities which carry out the theme of the play day.

Evaluation

Immediately after a play day is concluded, a complete evaluation should be made. This is how schools can improve and enrich the entire extramural offering. Furthermore, this is how students learn.

ORGANIZATION OF A PLAY DAY

Generally one person is placed in charge of all chairmen and their respective committees. The division of responsibilities for the committees may be as follows:

A. Invitation Committee
   1. Prepare and send invitations, which should include
      a. Date, time, place
      b. Registration fee (if any) for each student, team, or school
      c. Types of events
      d. Number of players to bring
      e. Requests for additional equipment such as ball, pinnies, etc.
      f. Deadline date for reply
   2. Prepare and send follow-up letter, which should include
      a. Complete game schedule
      b. Rules to be used and any modifications in playing areas, heights of nets, etc.

    c. Cost of refreshments, if any
    d. Exact time and place of registration
    e. Provision for officials, scorers, timers
    f. Telephone and address of chairman and faculty advisor
    g. Plans for entertainment

B. Reception Committee
    1. Act as hostesses
    2. Register and collect money
    3. Divide participants into teams; for this purpose they may be given
       a. Colored ribbons
       b. Name tags
       c. Cardboard cutouts representing the theme of the play day
    4. Check wraps, purses, etc.

C. Equipment Committee
    1. Gather and issue supplies
    2. Collect equipment
    3. Return equipment to correct people

D. Publicity Committee
    1. Send appropriate information to newspaper
    2. Announce the coming play day in classes
    3. Prepare bulletins
    4. Make appropriate bulletin boards (posters)
    5. Prepare a scrapbook or memory book of the event

E. Program and Theme Committee
    1. Choose the theme
    2. Plan the activities for the day, including mixers, relays and games
    3. Arrange for play leaders for each group

F. Officials
    1. Secure a head official
    2. Secure as many other officials as are necessary to conduct the various activities

G. Refreshment Committee
    1. Plan and provide refreshments
    2. Clean up

H. Entertainment Committee
    1. Plan and arrange for songs and cheers, skits from the participating groups
    2. Plan an appropriate activity for the hostess school to present

I. Evaluation Committee
   1. Contact faculty advisors and leaders from each participating school
      for an evaluation of the play day; this should be done immediately
   2. Conduct an evaluation of the play day by the chairmen and mem-
      bers of all committees from the hostess school

SPORTS DAYS

Sports days are generally organized and administered somewhat like
play days. The major exceptions are that teams from specific schools play
as a unit and the program usually consists of competition in one sport
only. This stimulates keener competition. Instead of centering the activities
of the day around some novel theme, the occasion is devoted to playing
one sport: Hockey Sports Day, Volleyball Sports Day, etc. Emphasis is
still placed on social and recreational objectives and the occasion concludes
with refreshments.

SOURCES OF AID

The American Association for Health, Physical Education and Recreation (AAHPER) includes, among others, two divisions: the Division
for Girls and Women's Sports, and the Division of Boys and Men's Athletics. Both have printed information about intramural and extramural
programs.

The Division for Girls and Women's Sports (DGWS) through the
AAHPER sponsors the Athletic and Recreation Federation of College
Women (ARFCW) from which Women's Recreation Associations (WRA)
and Girls Athletic Associations (GAA) can receive aid. Play days, sports
days and other extramural events are often a part of the program of these
organizations. Most high schools have a Girls Athletic Association or a Girls
Recreation Association. Most colleges and universities have a Women's Athletic Association, Women's Recreation Association, or a College or University Recreation Association (coeducational in nature).

The DGWS writes and compiles and the AAHPER publishes official
rules for girls' sports and pamphlets on standards for recreational
activities.

The American Association for Health, Physical Education and Recreation publishes material which gives specific assistance to officials and
players, help on the development of spectator sportsmanship, information
about recreational games, outdoor education, and values in sports. The
latter, written jointly by men and women, discusses the role of athletics
and sports in developing personal value systems. An excellent handbook
on girls' sports organizations is also available from this source.

The National Intramural Association has taken the lead in conducting institutes, holding conventions, and disseminating information about the programming of men's intramurals and extramurals.

The National Recreation Association, The American Recreation Society, The American Camping Association, and the magazines *Recreation* and *The Camping Magazine* offer wide sources of information.

Chapter 12

Leagues and Tournaments

There are many ways of dividing groups into competitive units or leagues. Competition may be between homerooms, classes, departments, majors, clubs, dormitories, schools, fraternities, or sororities. Teams can be chosen by captains. The most important point is to divide the participants into as nearly equal ability groups as possible.

In general, ability is best determined by achievement in a specific activity. For tennis competition, for example, performance in that game is the best indicator of tennis ability. If size or maturity is a factor and no knowledge of ability in the specific game in question is available, for example, in touch football, then a general classification system such as that of the California Interscholastic Federation may be used as a basis for dividing groups into teams (Figure 12.1).

After teams have been established, then the appropriate type of tournament must be selected. Selecting the proper tournament is essential for successful and enjoyable competition.

Handicapping is a method used to equalize the competition between contestants of unequal ability. It is seldom used in school intramural programs. Activities which readily lend themselves to handicapping, however, are golf, bowling, archery, and tennis. If information is needed about handicapping, consult the specific activity association rule book.

SINGLE ELIMINATION TOURNAMENT

The single elimination tournament is the simplest type of tournament to conduct. It requires little time, and is adaptable to large numbers of

Exponent	Grade	Age Yrs. Mos.	Height Inches	Weight Pounds	Classes
8		13	61	91	Class D
9		13-0- 5	61	91- 93	Sum of Exponents
10		13-6-11	62	94- 96	is 49 or less
11		14-0- 5	63	97- 99	
12	9	14-6-11	64	100-102	
13	10	15-0- 5	65	103-105	
14	11	15-6-11	66	106-108	Class C
15	12	16-0- 5	67	109-111	Sum of Exponents
16		16-6-11	68	112-114	is 50-56 incl.
17		17-0- 5	69	115-119	
18		17-6- 8	70 & Over	120-124	
19		17-9-11		125-129	
20		18-0- 2		130-134	Class B
21		18-3- 5		135-139	Sum of Exponents
22		18-6- 8		140-141	is 57-63 incl.
23		18-9-11		142-143	
24		19 & Over		144-145	
25				146-147	
26				148-149	Class A
27				150-151	Sum of Exponents
28				152-153	is 64 or more
29				154-155	
30				156 & Over	

Example:

Boy in Grade 9	- Exponent for grade is	12
Age 15 yrs. 3 mos.	- Exponent for age is	13
Height 66 inches	- Exponent for height is	14
Weight 120 pounds	- Exponent for weight is	18
	Sum of exponents (Class B)	57

CALIFORNIA SYSTEM FOR THE CLASSIFICATION OF HIGH
SCHOOL BOYS

Figure 12.1

participants. However, it has several disadvantages. Fifty per cent of the participants are eliminated after only one match. Obviously, the poorest players do not get much play in this type of tournament. This is discouraging to players. When the object is to secure as much participation as possible, as is the case in conducting school recreation programs, then the single elimination tournament is a poor choice. At the end of the tournament, there is only one winner and practically no ranking of teams. Unless the seeding is done carefully at the beginning, a good team may be eliminated quickly; consequently, the tournament finals may not really represent the two best teams. The single elimination is a good tournament for a particular purpose — that of determining one winner as soon as possible — but it has many disadvantages.

Rules for Setting Up Elimination Tournaments

Figure 12.2 indicates that eight teams are entered in this tournament. By observing Figure 12.2 one can conclude that the winning team must play three matches. For each additional bracket of teams entered in this kind of single elimination tournament play, one additional match would be required of the winning teams. Figure 12.3 indicates that the winning team would have to play four matches. If there were thirty-two teams entered in the tournament, the winning team would be required to play five matches; if sixty-four teams were entered the winning team would be required to play six matches.

Seeding of Teams

Teams or individuals for tournament play should be arranged so that the strongest or best teams are not eliminated in the first rounds of competition. Figures 12.2 and 12.4 indicate the placement of the four best teams, selected by previous records, by qualifying rounds, or, if neither of these is known, by assumed ability ranking.

Byes

When the number of individuals or teams entered in a single elimination tournament is not a perfect power of two, a number of byes are

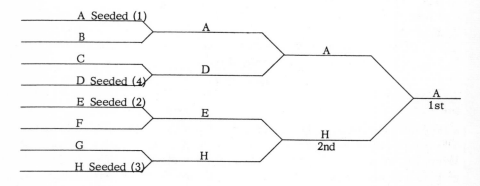

DIAGRAM SHOWING AN 8 TEAM STRAIGHT ELIMINATION TOURNAMENT
(Numbers After Letters Indicates Seeded Teams)

Figure 12.2

necessary in arranging for tournament play. Figures 12.3 and 12.4 indicate placement of byes. In some tournaments the qualifying rounds are used to reduce the number of contestants to a perfect power of two, thus eliminating the need for byes. It is always recommended that when possible single elimination tournaments be arranged so they comply with the rule, perfect power of two.

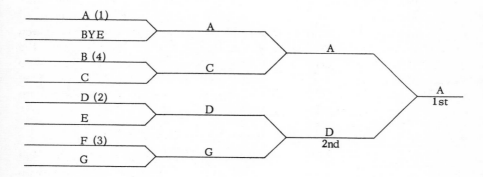

CORRECT ORGANIZATION OF AN ELIMINATION TOURNAMENT WHEN
THE NUMBER OF TEAMS IS NOT A PERFECT POWER OF TWO

Figure 12.3

Rounds

The first series of matches is referred to as the "first round of play." The second round of play in the diagram Figure 12.4 is referred to as the "quarter finals," the third as the "semifinals," and the fourth, the "finals."

DOUBLE ELIMINATION TOURNAMENT

The second-chance tournament has one distinct advantage over the preceding tournaments — a loser in any round may still play for the championship — if the team can win the rest of its games. The fact that the tournament results in a better placing of players at the end is another desirable aspect. On the other hand, this tournament takes longer to play and consequently is not suitable for all occasions.

The double elimination tournament is started in the same way as the single elimination tournament. After the first round of play, the losers, indicated by Figure 12.4 by broken lines, meet one another and continue the elimination as diagrammed. In this same figure, Teams A and F play

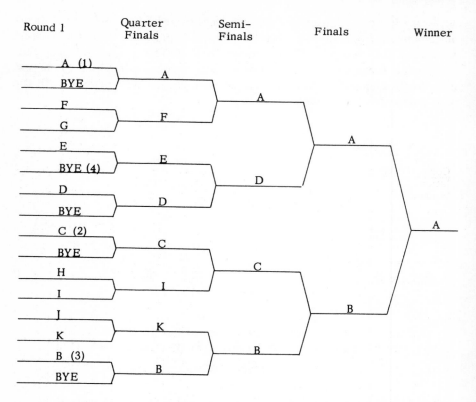

SINGLE ELIMINATION TOURNAMENT (16 BRACKETS — 11 TEAMS —
5 BYES) NUMBERS AFTER LETTERS INDICATE SEEDED TEAMS

Figure 12.4

the best two out of three contests to determine who will play Team G
for the championship.

By following the diagram in Figure 12.7, one can see how the losing
teams are arranged for further play when sixteen teams are entered in
a double elimination tournament. In this figure the losing teams move to
the left while the winning teams continue progress to the right of the
diagram.

ROUND ROBIN TOURNAMENT

The round robin is distinguished from all other tournaments by the
fact that each player or team of players plays each other player or team
of players in a definite order. In this tournament, participation is at a

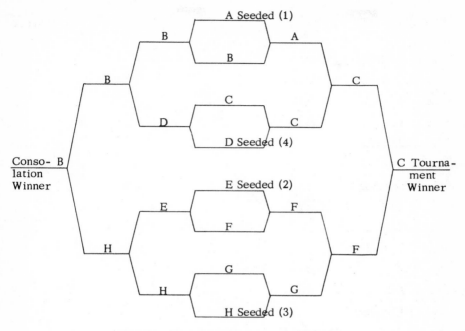

ELIMINATION — CONSOLATION TOURNAMENT

Figure 12.5

maximum. No team has an easier playing schedule than any other. At the close of this tournament, all teams are ranked in respective order, thus providing an objective measure of playing skill. There are, on the other hand, several disadvantages, the primary one being that the tournament takes a long time to complete. At the end, two or more teams may tie for a single place. This can be eliminated, however, by conducting a play-off between them. Because every team plays every other team, if there are many entries the time required to complete the round robin may be exorbitant. This can be avoided by conducting several small round robin tournaments simultaneously and then having the winners of each play for the championship.

The chief advantage of the round robin tournament over the elimination tournament is that the former permits a team to continue playing after it has been beaten, whereas in the elimination tournament a defeated team is barred automatically from competition. From an educational point of view, the round robin tournament is preferable.

In drawing up this style of round robin tournament, the first team remains in a fixed position while the others rotate. Note, for example, in

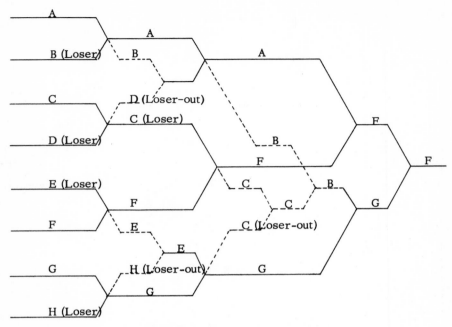

DOUBLE ELIMINATION TOURNAMENT

Figure 12.6

each of the leagues outlined in Figure 12.8 that Team 1 remains in the same position in every round. In the case of an odd number of teams, "X" or "bye" remains fixed and the teams rotate. The total number of games necessary to play off a round robin tournament is $\dfrac{N \times (N\text{-}1)}{2}$. If the number of teams is six, for example, it can be seen by substituting in the formula that it takes 15 games to complete the tournament

$$\left[\frac{6 \times (6\text{-}1)}{2} = \frac{30}{2} = 15 \right].$$

The schedule and score form in Figure 12.9 is used extensively throughout the United States. It is a simple, easy method of indicating outcomes of all contests within a league.

The percentage form shown in Figure 12.10 may be used to determine standings by percentages. As an example, a team with three losses and five wins would have a percentage standing of .625. On the other hand, a team with five losses and only three wins would have a percentage standing of .375.

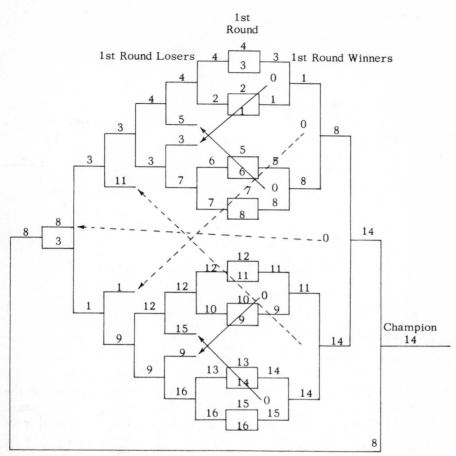

0 - Indicates Loser

DOUBLE ELIMINATION TOURNAMENT

Figure 12.7

LADDER TOURNAMENT

The ladder tournament is best used for conducting competition in individual or dual sports because it can be played off informally by contestants at their choice of time. If an individual tournament that can continue for a long time is desired, this is the tournament. Again it should be noted that a listed advantage may not be an advantage in all situations. This tournament must continue for quite a period of time in order to in-

<u>Round Robin Tournament</u>

Substitute the name of each team for a number and follow through with each round of play.

Four-Team League

Round I	II	III
1 vs 2	1 vs 3	1 vs 4
3 vs 4	2 vs 4	2 vs 3

Five-Team League

Round I	II	III	IV	V
1 vs X	1 vs 2	1 vs 3	1 vs 4	1 vs 5
2 vs 5	3 vs X	4 vs 2	5 vs 3	X vs 4
3 vs 4	4 vs 5	5 vs X	X vs 2	2 vs 3

Six-Team League

Round I	II	III	IV	V
1 vs 6	1 vs 2	1 vs 3	1 vs 4	1 vs 5
2 vs 5	3 vs 6	4 vs 2	5 vs 3	6 vs 4
3 vs 4	4 vs 5	5 vs 6	6 vs 2	2 vs 3

Seven-Team League

Round I	II	III	IV	V	VI	VII
1 vs X	1 vs 2	1 vs 3	1 vs 4	1 vs 5	1 vs 6	1 vs 7
2 vs 7	3 vs X	4 vs 2	5 vs 3	6 vs 4	7 vs 5	X vs 6
3 vs 6	4 vs 7	5 vs X	6 vs 2	7 vs 3	X vs 4	2 vs 5
4 vs 5	5 vs 6	6 vs 7	7 vs X	X vs 2	2 vs 3	3 vs 4

Eight-Team League

Round I	II	III	IV	V	VI	VII
1 vs 8	1 vs 2	1 vs 3	1 vs 4	1 vs 5	1 vs 6	1 vs 7
2 vs 7	3 vs 8	4 vs 2	5 vs 3	6 vs 4	7 vs 5	8 vs 6
3 vs 6	4 vs 7	5 vs 8	6 vs 2	7 vs 3	8 vs 4	2 vs 5
4 vs 5	5 vs 6	6 vs 7	7 vs 8	8 vs 2	2 vs 3	3 vs 4

Nine-Team League

Round I	II	III	IV	V	VI	VII
1 vs X	1 vs 2	1 vs 3	1 vs 4	1 vs 5	1 vs 6	1 vs 7
2 vs 9	3 vs X	5 vs 2	5 vs 3	6 vs 4	7 vs 5	8 vs 6
3 vs 8	4 vs 9	6 vs X	6 vs 2	7 vs 3	8 vs 4	9 vs 5
4 vs 7	5 vs 8	7 vs 9	7 vs X	8 vs 2	9 vs 3	X vs 4
5 vs 6	6 vs 7	8 vs 8	8 vs 9	9 vs X	X vs 2	2 vs 3

VIII	IX
1 vs 8	1 vs 9
9 vs 7	X vs 8
X vs 6	2 vs 7
2 vs 5	3 vs 6
3 vs 4	4 vs 5

ROUND ROBIN TOURNAMENT

Figure 12.8

Ten-Team League

Round I	II	III	IV	V	VI	VII
1 vs 10	1 vs 2	1 vs 3	1 vs 4	1 vs 5	1 vs 6	1 vs 7
2 vs 9	3 vs 10	4 vs 2	5 vs 3	6 vs 4	7 vs 5	8 vs 6
3 vs 8	4 vs 9	5 vs 10	6 vs 2	7 vs 3	8 vs 4	9 vs 5
4 vs 7	5 vs 8	6 vs 9	7 vs 10	8 vs 2	9 vs 3	10 ys 4
5 vs 6	6 vs 7	7 vs 8	8 vs 9	9 vs 10	10 vs 2	2 vs 3

VIII	IX
1 vs 8	1 vs 9
9 vs 7	10 vs 2
10 vs 6	8 vs 3
2 vs 5	7 vs 4
3 vs 4	6 vs 5

Eleven-Team League

Round I	II	III	IV	V	VI	VII
1 vs X	1 vs 2	1 vs 3	1 vs 4	1 vs 5	1 vs 6	1 vs 7
2 vs 11	3 vs X	4 vs 2	5 vs 3	6 vs 4	7 vs 5	8 vs 6
3 vs 10	4 vs 11	5 vs X	6 vs 2	7 vs 3	8 vs 4	9 vs 5
4 vs 9	5 vs 10	6 vs 11	7 vs X	8 vs 2	9 vs 3	10 vs 4
5 vs 8	6 vs 9	7 vs 10	8 vs 11	9 vs 10	10 vs 2	11 vs 3
6 vs 7	7 vs 8	8 vs 9	9 vs 10	10 vs 11	11 vs X	X vs 2

VIII	IX	X	XI
1 vs 8	1 vs 9	1 vs 10	1 vs 11
9 vs 7	10 vs 8	11 vs 9	X vs 10
10 vs 6	11 vs 7	X vs 8	2 vs 9
11 vs 5	X vs 6	2 vs 7	3 vs 8
X vs 4	2 vs 5	3 vs 6	4 vs 7
2 vs 3	3 vs 4	4 vs 5	5 vs 6

Figure 12.8 (Continued)

sure a proper ranking of players. One major advantage is that no players are eliminated, regardless of whether they win or lose.

The most skilled players, if known, are placed at the bottom. They have to work their way up the ladder; this generally stimulates increased interest in participation. The rules are rather simple. Generally one must challenge, and accept at least one challenge, each week. Usually one is permitted to challenge no more than two positions above his station on the ladder. Often the final date for play is posted when the tournament draw is posted.

PYRAMID TOURNAMENT

The pyramid tournament offers the same advantages and disadvantages as the ladder tournament. The chief difference is that you start with a wider base, and this gives more space from which to work. It is also

	1	2	3	4	5	6	7	8
1	X							
2	15-7	X		15-6				
3		9-15	X		15-13			
4		6-15		X	12-15			
5					X			
6						X		
7							X	
8								X

League____________________

1 ____________________ 5 ____________________

2 ____________________ 6 ____________________

3 ____________________ 7 ____________________

4 ____________________ 8 ____________________

ROUND ROBIN SCHEDULE AND SCORE FORM

Figure 12.9

Games Won

Games Lost	1	2	3	4	5	6	7	8	9	10	11	12	13	14	15
1	.500	.667	.750	.800	.833	.857	.875	.889	.900	.909	.917	.923	.929	.933	.938
2	.333	.500	.600	.667	.714	.750	.778	.800	.818	.833	.846	.857	.867	.875	.882
3	.250	.400	.500	.571	.625	.667	.700	.727	.750	.769	.786	.800	.813	.824	.833
4	.200	.333	.428	.500	.556	.600	.636	.667	.692	.714	.733	.750	.764	.778	.789
5	.167	.286	.375	.444	.500	.545	.583	.615	.643	.667	.688	.706	.722	.737	.750
6	.143	.250	.333	.400	.455	.500	.538	.571	.600	.625	.647	.667	.684	.700	.714
7	.125	.222	.300	.364	.417	.462	.500	.533	.563	.588	.611	.633	.650	.667	.682
8	.111	.200	.273	.333	.385	.428	.467	.500	.529	.556	.579	.600	.619	.636	.652
9	.100	.182	.250	.308	.357	.400	.438	.471	.500	.526	.550	.571	.591	.609	.625
10	.091	.167	.231	.286	.333	.375	.412	.444	.474	.500	.524	.545	.565	.583	.600
11	.083	.154	.214	.267	.313	.353	.389	.421	.450	.476	.500	.522	.542	.560	.576
12	.077	.143	.200	.250	.294	.333	.368	.400	.428	.455	.478	.500	.520	.538	.556
13	.071	.133	.188	.235	.278	.316	.350	.381	.408	.435	.458	.480	.500	.519	.536
14	.067	.125	.176	.222	.263	.300	.333	.364	.391	.417	.440	.462	.481	.500	.517
15	.063	.118	.167	.211	.250	.286	.318	.348	.375	.400	.423	.444	.464	.483	.500

PERCENTAGE FORM

Figure 12.10

Lynch 1

Maurer 2

Shutt 3

Mills 4

Loring 5

Spray 6

Klein 7

Smith 8

Mazzola 9

Harrison 10

Erickson 11

Hall 12

LADDER TOURNAMENT

Figure 12.11

easier to involve a larger number of contestants than in the ladder tournament. Additional advantages are that no one individual is on the bottom step by himself, and the arrangement affords a number of contestants to challenge. This aids players in getting past an opponent who seems to have "their number." Otherwise the playing rules for the pyramid and ladder tournaments are the same.

BRIDGE TOURNAMENT

The bridge tournament is best adapted to instructional and recreational situations in which dual sports are being played. It provides a

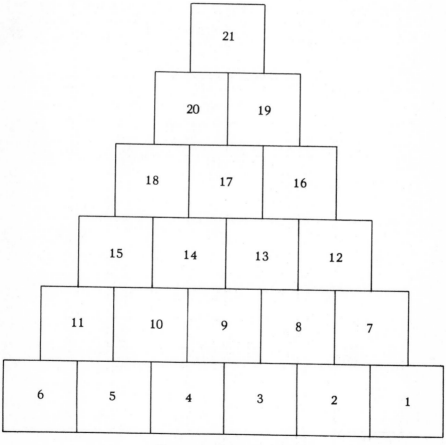

PYRAMID TOURNAMENT

Figure 12.12

friendly and sociable type of tournament, and is very informal in nature. The leader can start and conclude this tournament at will. It lends itself, therefore, to short periods of time very easily. Its one main disadvantage is that it results in no uncontested winner, yet this is what makes this tournament so much fun. It is most suitable for tennis, volleyball, badminton, and table tennis.

Several different rules of play may be used in the bridge tournament. Often the winning teams rotate at the end of a given period, as indicated in Figure 12.13. The aggregate score may be used to determine the winning team.

MARKER TOURNAMENT

The marker tournament is a good long-range tournament that is best suited for informal situations. It is like the bridge tournament in this regard. The players are given a certain goal to reach. In bowling, for ex-

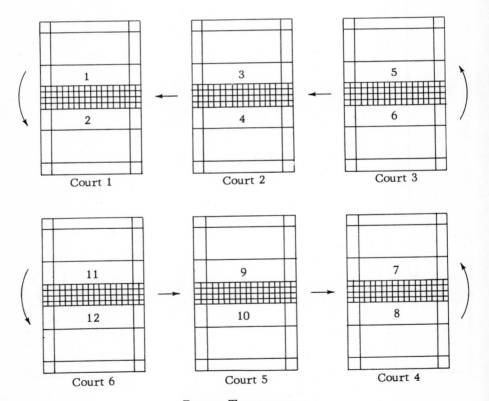

BRIDGE TOURNAMENT

Figure 12.13

ample, each player may be required to achieve one thousand points. Each time he bowls he therefore totals his scores until he has one thousand points. The best player, bowling around two hundred, obviously will achieve the set goal before the player who has a hard time scoring one hundred.

This tournament may also be scored on a team score basis. A team may total each of its individual member's scores to make the team score. This tournament offers many possibilities. It is an excellent motivational device and provides considerable freedom. It therefore makes a good tournament for college or adult recreational competition.

UNUSUAL TYPES OF TOURNAMENTS

Occasionally intramural directors have used additional less-known types of tournaments. A brief description of these tournaments follows.

King, or Crown, tournament consists of a triangle of pyramids. The same rules, advantages, and disadvantages of the pyramid tournament apply to this tournament.

The *Funnel* tournament resembles a pyramid with a ladder projecting from its apex. It permits a broad base at the bottom with several single ranking positions at the top. Otherwise the rules, advantages, and disadvantages are similar to those applying to the ladder and pyramid tournaments.

The *Tombstone* tournament consists of a best score, marks, or accomplishments in the shortest period of time. It is very similar to the Marker tournament.

Round-the-Clock tournament is similar to the ladder in many respects. The winner is determined by seeing which participant can advance a complete revolution from his starting position. Players may challenge up to three positions in advance of their stations.

Ringer tournaments are similar to the marker and are used as a challenge to accumulate the highest score possible in an activity in a given period of time.

Telegraphic, Telephone, and *Postal* tournaments are used when contestants from one school wish to challenge those from a different part of the country, and where travel for face-to-face competition is not possible. Competition is based upon prearranged rules. Activities most suitable for this type of competition are bridge, golf, archery, bowling, horseshoes, swimming, and track.

POINT SYSTEMS

Perhaps the greatest variances in intramural programs lie in their point systems. The point system should be one that tends to equalize the opportunities for all teams, leagues, and clubs that enter into the program. After the point program has been established it should be mimeographed and given to each participating unit, along with all basic rules.

It is possible to develop a good intramural program without benefit of either awards or point systems. It is usually beneficial to use both, however.

In schools where there are well established clubs, fraternities, sororities, or other organizations it is the usual practice to have a point system. A certain number of points are given to each participating unit for entering an activity; additional points are given to first, second, third, and fourth place winners. Additional points can be earned for services rendered by members of participating units, such as referees, umpires, scorers, reporters, and timers. Points are frequently awarded as follows (it will be noticed that more points are awarded for team than for individual participation):

Activity	Entrance Points	1st Pl.	2nd Pl.	3rd Pl.	4th Pl.
Basketball	50	150	125	100	75
Swimming (must enter five men to secure maximum entry points)	50	100	80	60	40
Volleyball	50	150	125	100	75
Tennis	25	50	40	30	20
Badminton	25	50	40	30	20
Handball	25	50	40	30	20
Bowling (must enter five-man team to secure maximum points)	25	50	40	30	20
Golf	25	50	40	30	20
Track (must enter five men)	50	100	80	60	40
Softball	50	150	125	100	75
Table Tennis	25	50	40	30	20
Two-man Volleyball	25	50	40	30	20

Individual points are frequently awarded in intramural programs, a practice approved by many people. Individual points may be awarded on the following basis: One point is given to each player who participates as much as two consecutive minutes in any team, dual, or individual sport. A limit of ten points per entry should be placed on each specific activity. In track and field and swimming meets, points are usually awarded as follows: five points for first place, three points for second place, two points for third place, one point for fourth place.

ENTRY FORMS AND SCORE SHEETS

Entry forms that lead to clear, accurate information eliminate hours of needless work in administering an intramural program. Every effort should be made to provide entry blanks that are easy to fill out, yet which are comprehensive enough to permit recording of all necessary information. Entry forms should provide for the following information: entry date, time of play, special rules, type of tournament, name, address, and phone number of each participant. A large number of forms, charts, and guide sheets are included in the Appendix as samples.

Chapter 13

Eligibility, Awards, and Promotion of Recreational Activities

The strength and vitality of school recreation, particularly its intramural-extramural aspects, are partly dependent on the established rules and practices that govern eligibility, awards, and promotion of the program. The rules must be clear, concise, simple, and few in number. When any question arises concerning, for example, the eligibility of a student, the forfeiture of a contest, or the awarding of points, the question should be answered immediately by using previously established rules. A copy of the pertinent facts should be made available to each participant. If this is not possible, the next best thing is to post the rules where everyone can see them.

ELIGIBILITY

Most schools have eligibility rules for interscholastic events but permit almost any student to take part in the general recreation program. This is for all students, and rules which tend to keep them out of the program defeat its purpose. Consequently, there should be few eligibility regulations. The only exceptions might be those pertaining to violations of school disciplinary rules, school scholastic standards, or requirements that all contestants who engage in active physical recreation successfully pass a physical examination. Students should participate in only a reasonable number of activities; overparticipation and misplacement of values are as unfortunate as no participation.

Customarily, high schools and colleges hold to the idea of barring lettermen from intramural participation in sports in which they have won varsity awards unless there are openings on the team and the principle of equality can be applied; for example, one letterman might be allowed on each team. It is often more advantageous, however, to utilize their services as volunteer coaches or game officials. The latter plan seems to be the better one, as the use of trained professional coaches sometimes makes intramural competition too competitive. Following are some tested, easy-to-enforce rules:

1. Varsity lettermen are ineligible to compete in intramural athletics in the sports in which they have lettered.
2. All students who participate in varsity, junior varsity, or freshmen athletics during the current school year are ineligible to compete in intramural athletics in the sport in which they participate.
3. All freshmen and junior varsity lettermen are ineligible to compete in the sport in which they lettered unless they have stayed out of competition for one year.
4. Participants must be students in good standing who are carrying at least one-half load of academic work.
5. Water polo and cross-country competition are considered as swimming and track participations, respectively, and are governed by the foregoing rules.
6. All participants must be on the active roll list in the recreation office.
7. Persons already graduated are not eligible to participate in the organized phase of the competitive program.
8. Should a team, club, sorority, or fraternity use an ineligible player it loses all points — both entrance and placement points in that particular activity.
9. In order to earn entry points, participating units must appear and play in at least the first scheduled round of the activity.
10. All entries must be made on time and accompanied by entry fees (if they are charged).
11. Participants must show up with a full team, ready to play within 10 minutes of the scheduled time, else they lose by forfeit.
12. If neither team fails to appear, the match is scored as a double forfeit.

AWARDS

Should awards be given? What constitutes a good award? As far as we know, it has always been customary for victors to receive tangible evidence of their success. Sometimes substantial material awards of wealth, position, decoration, or power have been bestowed upon champions. Amateurism and good sportsmanship often have been forfeited as contestants have been encouraged by unscrupulous persons to stoop to any means in order to win. To vie for awards of great material value is opposed in spirit to the high ideals which can be fostered by healthy competition. The ancient Greek symbol of Olympic victory was merely an olive wreath. Such a token symbolized success but by the nature of the wreath the suggestion was made that competitive glory is short-lived; victory is temporal. The contestant gives all that he has but does not expect material award for his efforts. This ancient Grecian custom is appropriate today and inexpensive symbolic awards are a popular and sufficient stimulation for school recreational efforts. A good award need not be expensive. Awards should be given at the time they are won, else their effectiveness may be lost. Special display cases for the awards are good means of sharpening the desire for competition in advance of the actual contest. These cases should be placed where all may see the cups, ribbons, and/or other awards.

The most common individual awards are *letters*, which are available in various colors and sizes; since they can be worn they are most popular; *certificates*, but today these are not too popular; *medals and charms*, which are frequently given and are generally satisfactory; *sweaters*, though these awards are generally too expensive for intramural budgets; and *ribbons*, which are awards and one of the best liked.

The most common group awards include *cups*, which are expensive, but they are permanent and are especially good for "traveling" or "perpetual" awards; and *plaques*, which are popular, inexpensive and can be made of wood.

PUBLICITY

To be successful, the recreation program must be attractive and interesting. To achieve this goal, devices which capture attention, create enthusiasm, and provide information must be utilized. Good publicity is one of these devices. This includes all measures taken to present recreational opportunities to the students and faculty and all efforts made toward securing understanding of the program.

It is advantageous to center all publicity which is to go to newspapers in one person's hands, or, if the program is a large one, a publicity bureau can be responsible for this aspect of the program. This manner of operation is more organized and certainly news channels prefer it. If too many individuals attempt to secure publicity, confusing and conflicting information may be given; also, since everyone's business may become no one's responsibility, many important and interesting announcements may never be made.

Newspapers like pictures and photographs of anything that is of unusual interest.

Most departments find it helpful to print a handbook containing information about their program. The school annual can be utilized and may contain the names of winners and numerous action photographs. Informational material should be submitted to news bureaus well in advance; it should be accurate and complete, giving all pertinent facts: complete homes, places, dates, scores, outstanding features.

Bulletin boards can be made attractive, interesting, and informative. Special attention should be given to the arrangement of captions to attract students to stop and read them. Students having specific artistic skills should be recruited or others taught this important assignment. In fact, in many schools, bulletin boards are considered the best device for stimulating interest in and promoting the school recreation program.

Posters are successfully utilized by many schools to promote the program. If the school has its own print shop the expense for this type of publicity is negligible. If outside printing agencies have to be utilized, however, the cost may be prohibitive if posters are used extensively. "Print it yourself" kits are being effectively used by some recreation departments. Their greatest drawback is that they are extremely time-consuming to make.

If students who have drawing, printing, and caricaturing skills are recruited, the utilization of various posters for all phases of the recreation program may be most rewarding.

Handbooks are used extensively by colleges and universities to acquaint students with all phases of the recreational program. This device has not, however, been used by many public elementary and secondary schools.

Most handbooks give a complete description of how all recreational activities are organized and supervised. Usually the handbooks are printed annually and present an account of the previous year's activities with pictures of the winning teams and other interesting highlights of the program.

The use of handbooks is highly recommended if the cost of publication is not prohibitive. Departments anticipating original use of this device should secure sample copies from schools which have already established acceptable layouts for their publication.

Additional devices successfully used by various schools to publicize their recreation program are printed bulletins, handbills, class and assembly announcements, student yearbooks, play days, play nights, motion pictures, photography, radio, open house, and various exhibitions.

Chapter 14

Special Interest Clubs

Civilized man has always been interested in banding together with others who enjoy the same hobbies or who engage in the same leisure-time occupations. Groups often have centered around the arts, sports, literary activities, nature study, or collecting. Today it is usual in every large community to find clubs devoted to crafts, drama, music, dance, sports, camping, horseback riding, hunting, fishing, flying, stamp collecting, painting, nature study, cycling, books, chess, bridge, and a host of other topics.

The school is one of the principal agencies equipped and staffed to sponsor special interest clubs. An exposure to some of these activities during school years may well "infect" students with lasting enthusiasm that will influence their lives.

ORGANIZING A CLUB

Generally, school clubs are formed in the following manner. The recreation director uses whatever promotional media he has to acquaint students with the possibility of organizing a special interest activity. Perhaps the most common forms of publicity are:

1. Pamphlets that outline the general purpose of the club.
2. School and community newspapers in which the major purposes of the club are described.
3. Posters on the bulletin boards.
4. Class and assembly announcements.
5. Word-of-mouth communication.

When an adequate number responds, the interested persons are called together to consider the proposal. The director then discusses the general purposes of the club with those who have expressed interest. He informs them of any pertinent school regulations regarding group activities. If the students are interested in the proposal they proceed by agreeing on the following: name of the club, time and place for meetings, membership regulations, officers needed, and choice of sponsor.

The director's functions are those of organizing, administering and encouraging; of securing needed equipment and space; of finding a specialist who is sufficiently interested and capable of leading each special interest club.

The Sponsor

Often the recreation director can recommend certain faculty members or parents who have specific interests in an activity. The recreation director or the students then approach that person and invite him to become the club sponsor.

It is important that the sponsor have real interest in the specific club. He also should have certain attributes and characteristics conducive to leadership in the specific activity. In all situations, however, the sponsor should be friendly, understanding, and helpful to the students in all of the club endeavors. If the sponsor is a model worth emulating, membership in the organization will be a rich social experience.

Club Officers

The sponsor of the club or the recreation director discusses with the club members the general requirements and responsibilities of the officers. Most clubs need a president, vice-president, secretary, and treasurer.

Constitution

One of the first tasks of a newly formed club is to develop a simple constitution. The document generally defines the aims and purposes of the organization, gives the name of the club, the qualifications for membership, time and place of the meetings, the names and duties of officers, when and how these officers are to be selected, and makes provisions for amendments.

Progressive and dynamic clubs usually find it advisable to create various committees such as constitution committee, program committee, refreshment committee, clean-up committee, equipment committee, finance committee, publicity committee, and promotion committee.

Parliamentary Techniques

It is the responsibility of the recreation director to insure adequate in-service training for all club officers. They should be impressed with the necessity of conducting all meetings in a businesslike manner. Unless meetings are conducted by some definite parliamentary procedure, they often fail to accomplish the desired results. *Robert's Rules of Order* is the usual guide.

The agenda for each meeting should follow a given plan which includes:

1. The call to order
2. Reading of the minutes of the last meeting
3. Committee reports
4. Old business
5. New business
6. Announcements
7. Adjournment

TYPES OF CLUBS

Although the possibilities of special interests around which a club can be built are endless, it may be helpful to explore the hypothetical and particular considerations in establishing several types of clubs.

Music Club

Music has frequently been referred to as the "universal language." It is also probably one of the most universal forms of recreation, suitable for all levels of ability, all age groups and either sex, separately or together. In the formation of a music club, as in others, there should be no barriers of race or creed.

Due to the wide appeal of music and its many possibilities, a club could be organized around any one of several different phases of this activity. Emphasis could be placed on listening to music — symphonic, vocal, an instrumental group, popular or a combination of these — or it could be placed on making music of any of these types.

Let us consider some of the things a club could do.

MUSIC APPRECIATION CLUB.   After interest has been promoted in forming a music appreciation club, and at the first meeting of the interested group the director should be prepared to acquaint the students with several interesting possibilities for club activity. He should not dictate the course of action but should help the students to arrive at a good point of departure.

All too frequently, students are unaware of the many opportunities for listening to good music. Furthermore, they often lack sufficient knowledge to appreciate what they hear. If this is the case, the director will need to guide the choice of possible activities so that learning can take place.

Special Interest Clubs

Considerable interest can be developed in a music appreciation club regardless of the musical talent of its individual members. Membership should therefore be open to all those having any desire for this kind of activity.

At the first official meeting of the music club, it may be advisable to acquaint the students with opportunities for listening to "live" and recorded music. Some attention also should be given to determining the purposes and desires of the group and to ascertaining their general level of musical knowledge and sophistication. A study of the development of nonharmonic musical structure, for example, might be a stimulating recreational pursuit for some groups but probably would spell "finis" to many others.

It is well known that a great many people enjoy listening to music in spite of the fact that they have no academic knowledge of the basic elements of composition. Many persons, on the other hand, really do not know how to listen to music at all. To appreciate music fully, and to receive maximum pleasure from listening to it, one needs to understand first that it is composed of sound and movement. The basic elements of all music are rhythm, melody, form, and tone color. The music appreciation club could choose to learn "how to listen" and then make a study of each of the aforementioned elements.

A study of the characteristic tone color of each musical instrument may be used as an example. Through this study club members could obtain an understanding of the place and importance of each instrument in a band or symphony orchestra. For study purposes, musical instruments are usually grouped as follows:

1. Stringed instruments. There are four basic types of stringed instruments:
   a. *Bowed* (violin, viola, cello, bass viol)
   b. *Plucked* (harp, banjo, guitar, lute family, lyre, mandolin, ukelele, zither)
   c. *Hammered* (clavichord, dulcimer)
   d. *Wind* (Aeolian harp)
2. Woodwinds (flute, piccolo, oboe, English horn, clarinet, bass clarinet, bassoon, contra bassoon, saxophone)
3. Brasses (trumpet, trombone, tuba, French horn, flugelhorns, bugle, cornet)
4. Percussion. These instruments are usually divided into two basic types:
   a. Those that play definite notes (kettledrums, chimes, glockenspiel, marimba, orchestra bells, and the xylophone)
   b. Those that produce indefinite notes (drums, castanets, cymbals, gongs, tambourines, triangle)

5. Keyboard (piano, harpischord, celesta)
6. Other instruments. The following instruments do not belong to any of the previously listed categories: accordion, concertina, harmonica, bagpipes, flageolet, and ocarina.

The characteristics of each of the aforementioned groups of instruments may be noted by studying both live and recorded music. A music appreciation club may specialize in studying one specific type of music, or its members may gain more by choosing more than one. Ballet, chamber, choral, concertos, opera, musical comedy, folk music, jazz, and children's story records are some of the possibilities.

VOCAL MUSIC. Singing is probably the most natural form of musical participation. Music club members are generally interested in some form of group singing, informal or formal choral work, rather than in solo singing. They may specialize in any or a combination of the following groupings: mixed chorus, girls' glee club, boys' glee club, different kinds of choirs, madrigal singers, or smaller ensembles such as quartets. Members may wish to specialize in particular kinds of songs, such as folk, hymns, spirituals,

patriotic, popular, music of a chosen era, or music written by selected composers. In each case, consideration must be given to securing a rehearsal room, time, a competent director, appropriate music, and an accompanist. The group will sooner or later wish to explore opportunities for public performance.

INSTRUMENTAL MUSIC CLUB. Unless the recreation director has the techniques and skills of a music specialist, he will confine his efforts to the administrative and publicity phases and will place the directing, teaching, and coordinating of this activity in the hands of a specialist. There are, of course, many qualfied specialists in this field, and most schools do form instrumental music clubs which concentrate on any one of the following: orchestra, band, rhythm band, chamber music, concert band, marching band, and dance band.

The Drama Club

Frequently the dramatic club is one of the easiest to organize for it seems that most students have an unsatisfied desire to participate in make-believe situations. The recreation director thus should have little trouble in promoting this well-accepted activity. Dramatic materials appropriate for almost all age groups are available and easy to obtain for school use.

Dramatics are rich in personal rewards: fun for the participant, opportunity for creative self-expression and development of personality, development of graceful carriage, good speech, good posture, and poise in front of groups. Generally the dramatic club members learn useful, practical skills while making props, building sets, serving as light and sound technicians, printing programs, making costumes, and selecting and applying make-up properly. In addition there are worthwhile educational experiences in selecting plays, learning parts, casting, advertising, auditioning, and in countless other organizational and promotional phases of the club's activity.

An important point in making the offerings of the dramatic club successful is for the club to recognize its own limitations in ability to perform and to handle all of the essential details of production. If the recreation director guides the group carefully in its selection of plays, the members are almost certain to have pleasant and profitable experiences in dramatics.

Arts and Crafts Club

Like music, arts and crafts have universal appeal as special interest activities. Degree of talent, age, and even physical condition impose no important limitations on participation. There are opportunities for unlimited creativity and cultural growth within the reach of everyone.

For the elementary school age child there are simple crafts projects such as spatter prints, party decorations, dolls and their clothing, scrapbooks, leather, felt, and tooled copper projects, kites, wooden toys, and lanyards.

Nature crafts also are ideal for children. Through this medium they learn to use imagination in making countless objects from nature's waste products. Some of the most usual nature craft objects are pine-needle whisk brooms and dolls, woven table mats, small baskets, lapel ornaments, pine-cone birds and animals, seed necklaces, palm-leaf hats, ink prints or plaster casts of leaves or animal and bird tracks, clay models, mineral and rock mounts, and shell ornaments.

The high school group tends to be interested in oil and watercolor painting, tooled leather projects, loom weaving, art metal craft, model airplanes, sketching, needlework, rug making, stenciling, block printing, etching, and jewelry making.

In addition to practical work, secondary and college level students may wish to undertake the study of theoretical aspects of art as special club projects. Color harmony, for example, could be a fascinating topic with implications for home planning, the selection of clothing, and landscaping. The effect of color on the emotions is another subject rich in possibilities. People are not as superstitious about colors as they once were, but we are well aware that appetites, emotions, and moods are definitely influenced by colors. The effects that different colors are supposed to create may be brought to mind by using current idioms such as "in the red," "blue Monday," "true blue," "blue music," "blackmail," "blackball," "once in a blue moon," "white all the way through." As with other clubs, the direction the group takes and the intensity of interest will depend upon the particular students, locality, and leadership of the recreation director. Poor financial support and inadequate facilities and equipment can be compensated for to a large extent by a lively imagination in planning the program for the arts and crafts club.

Dance Club

The dance club tends to be one of the most popular high school and college special interest activities. It affords an excellent opportunity for socializing, making new friends, exercising, learning a fine carry-over activity, and in general having a good time.

The club members may choose to specialize in one kind of dance, such as modern or ballet, which is particularly appealing to girls. Coeducational groups more often include some combination of square, folk, social, tap, and round dancing in their club activities.

If the club members develop adequate skills, there are countless opportunities for participation in festivals and exhibitions. A recreational

dance group in Los Angeles, California, the Westchester Lariats, has traveled throughout the western hemisphere giving many performances before all kinds of audiences.

Aquatics Club

An aquatics club is another favorite on school campuses. Individual clubs often emphasize one or more of the following activities.

1. Red Cross certification in lifesaving or water safety
2. Presentation of synchronized swimming or water ballet
3. Canoeing, sailing, or crew

4. Skin and scuba diving
5. Surfing or water skiing
6. Speed swimming
7. Form swimming and diving

The inclusion of an aquatics club in the school recreation program usually is a gratifying practice. The activities are so inherently interesting that some success is assured even with a minimum of imaginative leadership. No matter how uncreative the leader, however, it is essential that safety rules be strictly adhered to at all times.

In summary, the five different special interest clubs discussed in this chapter are but a few of the many projects that could be initiated in almost any school. Other examples of possibilities are clubs focusing on chess, checkers, bridge, any of the sports, flying, gardening, books, and so on. The range is so great that the recreation director should be cautioned never to permit organization of more clubs and projects than can be properly supervised. In general, these club activities should be viewed as laboratory experiences where students learn to improve their cultural, educational, and social skills. In the end, the by-products of these experiences should enrich living.

Chapter 15

Special School Recreational Activities

Organized school recreational programs cover innumerable areas of interest. Some of the most popular include special events, camping and outdoor education projects, and school assembly programs. Often these particular activities are left unstructured and weakly supervised. As a result, the educational values which can accrue from these worthwhile experiences have not always been realized. On the other hand, special recreational activities can be most profitable and, if so, they well may be remembered longer than much of what happens in the academic classroom. Since these events are much desired by students, school authorities should capitalize on this golden opportunity and tie in with each experience every possible educational concept and relationship. Some values can be captured here that never can be approached in the classroom, and some of the learnings may make what otherwise seems to be dead subject matter come to life. It therefore is recommended that organization and supervision of these activities be formally assigned, possibly to the recreation director. He in turn should be held responsible for organizing them in such a way that all possible values can be derived from them.

SPECIAL EVENTS

This term includes scheduled activities, events, or projects that occur infrequently such as Hallowe'en celebrations; circuses; school carnivals; songfests; Easter egg hunts; special dance nights like the Senior Prom; Homecoming; May Day programs; Tom Sawyer fishing, and rodeos. Different special events are popular in varying sections of the country. It would be impractical as well as impossible to list all of the specific details involved in sponsoring these events. School size, location, grade level, the degree and extent of faculty and community support determine to a large extent how any one of these programs would be organized. Furthermore, it would defeat part of the purpose of these events to outline them in detail even if it were possible to do so for it is an educational experience for the faculty and students to plan this kind of activity for themselves. A few general ideas about the organization of special events should, however, be kept in mind. These are:

1. School special event programs afford wonderful opportunities in giving a large number of students valuable experiences in leadership.
2. All special events should be recreational in nature, that is, fun to do, but they should have maximum educational carry-over.
3. Each event should be conducted in such a way that maximum learnings result.
4. Every possible precaution should be taken to prevent accidents and to assure maximum safety for participants and spectators.
5. There should be an evaluative follow-up meeting at the conclusion of each special event.

CAMPING AND OUTDOOR EDUCATION PROJECTS

Since the days of Pestalozzi, Rousseau, and Froebel, educational philosophers have encouraged teachers to use outdoor educational projects. At long last, hundreds of school districts throughout the United Staates now have extended classroom activities, and thousands of students attend school camps for different periods of time.

In 1872 organized outdoor education had its meager beginning at Camp Chautauqua. Since that time, and largely due to the support of the W. K. Kellogg Foundation, school camping and outdoor education projects have become an integral part of countless elementary school curriculums throughout the United States.

Most school authorities seem to be satisfied with the abilities and competencies of their camp personnel. They are, however, dissatisfied with the pre-camp preparation of the children. It is believed that the children would receive greater values from outdoor education experiences if they had at least some knowledge of geology, astronomy, topography, forestry, wild life, conservation, and nature study before going to camp. Students usually know so little about these areas that, other than socially, they may gain little from the school camping experience. In addition to some knowledges of this sort, a tying-together of appropriate materials from the

courses in which the students are enrolled would contribute immeasurably to the camp experience. In addition, the following phase of the school camping experience needs a complete revamping to make the entire program more meaningful.

The program in too many school camps consists merely of ineffective puttering in crafts, weather study, nature study and conservation; inadequate discussions of the size and position of various celestial bodies, and some very bookish reports on rocks and minerals. Considerable time is spent on cooperative work projects, recreational games, and socialization. Often it appears that the program consists only of unstructured busy work or the regular formal school work is merely transposed from the school to the camp locale.

To be most effective, the outdoor education experience should consist of activities that can best be performed in camp situations; unfortunately, this is not necessarily the practice.

At their level of understanding, students should be acquainted with basic fundamentals of all phases of nature. This should be done in such a way that they become not only aware but keenly interested in and curious about the origin of the most minute aspects of their environment.

Units of study should include the formation of soil, rocks, mountains, valleys, and all aspects of erosion. The growth and recognition of trees, vegetation, and all forms of available plant life should be studied, examined, and related to life benefits and necessities. A comprehensive study should be made of the characteristics of local wildlife, including animals, fish, birds, and insects. School camping and outdoor education should become a most fruitful school experience.

SCHOOL ASSEMBLY PROGRAMS

There are several ways one might describe school assembly programs. Their origin seems to date back to the time when spiritual singing, prayer, and scripture reading were basic parts of every school's daily program. Lately it has become a time when extracurricular activities are conducted and presented by the students and faculty for the purpose of unifying and enriching school life. More specifically, it is a place and time where all the students meet, general announcements are made, and occasionally something worthwhile occurs. It is often the poorest planned and most wasted part of the school day.

Assembly programs should be organized in such a way that they are enlightening and enriching aspects of school life. Considerable time and thought should go into planning this extraclass activity. It should be used for the following purposes:

1. As a hub around and through which school activities center and school unification develops
2. As a showcase for school and worthwhile outside talent
3. As an aid in creating new interests and in furthering existing ones
4. As a place in which to develop the habits and attitudes of an intelligent audience
5. As an instrument in the development of school pride, a feeling of belonging and respect for the dignity of man
6. As a place to include worthwhile educational activities that fall outside the regular curriculum
7. As a place where important announcements are made and school policies are reviewed
8. As a place to share information and reserve guidance along vocational and ethical lines
9. As a place where recognition is given for excellence
10. As a place where students can develop poise, expression, ability, and responsibility through their own participation

Each assembly period should be interesting, stimulating, uplifting, and therefore valuable to both students and faculty. If such are the outcomes, then everyone will want to attend. To achieve these purposes, it is recommended that each school appoint an assembly committee made up of students and faculty. Their responsibilities would be to oultine a yearly calendar of assembly programs, set up purposes, guidelines, and regulations for them, and constantly re-evaluate programs in an effort to improve them. Other responsibilities of the assembly committee would be to determine program length, for if they are too short, they are disappointing and if they are too long they may be disrupting. The assembly committee should make sure that homeroom teachers discuss with students (not just tell them) their behavioral responsibilities. Occasionally it may be essential for the homeroom teacher to prepare the students for special assembly programs so they can obtain maximum values from the experience. The assembly committee should recommend when this should be done. The assembly committee should pre-screen all talent shows, movies, rallies, musicals, and outside talent exhibitions to see that nothing appears that is embarrassing and that the time is profitably spent.

The recreation director could be an excellent chairman or member of the assembly committee. He also could assume some other school responsibilities such as making the basic arrangements for most field trips and excursions; coordinating student activities at all athletic contests, plays, open houses, and other similar occasions; organizing and coordinating the school graduation programs; and acting as a clearing house for facilities requested by the community.

Special school recreational activities afford a treasure of untapped possibilities for cultural growth and development, waiting only for farsighted leadership with emphasis on organization and supervision.

Chapter 16

Public Relations

. . . with public sentiment nothing can fail; without it nothing can succeed. Consequently he who molds public opinion goes deeper than he who enacts statutes or pronounces decisions. He makes statutes and decisions possible to enact.
—ABRAHAM LINCOLN

Good public relations is the art of winning public favor. The term includes all of the activities connected with interpreting and improving the relationships of an organization or of an individual with the public. Thus, public relations is more than a narrow set of rules; it is the creation of an image. When the concept of service is presented in an acceptable way, it tends to create a halo effect, or favorable impression. This impression is needed in order to gain public support for school recreation.

For a long time we assumed that our recreation programs would speak for themselves and that the values were self-evident. Consequently little concerted effort was made to build a sound public relations program. It has become obvious, however, that we cannot assume that people will participate in our leisure-time programs nor expect them automatically to comprehend the need or understand the values of sound recreation. If we are to accomplish what we potentially can, we must sell our programs to the public.

METHODS USED IN PUBLIC RELATIONS

Innumerable methods are used in our technological, competitive age to create a desirable public image. Techniques and devices which are employed by recreation educators, however, must depend upon the specific situation and upon the facilities and media available. The methods listed here are applicable to most situations.

A. *Verbal*. Perhaps the best method of selling anything is by word of mouth. This is certainly true in school recreation. School recreation programs that are good will be enthusiastically talked about by the participants who engage in them and by the faculty and parents who witness them. It is necessary, however, to constantly keep the program in potential participant's minds via additional means. Announcement of current activities should be made in school assemblies, homeroom, and teachers' meetings. Over-all aspects of the whole program should be presented in orientation discussions. No one is more interested in the total growth and welfare of students than are parents; the need for recreation and the opportunities afforded by the school recreation program should be continuously presented to Parent Teachers Associations, Rotary and Lions clubs, church and other interested and influential groups. Recreation directors need to learn how to work cooperatively with the press and how to present good stories, how to use intercom and public address systems well. They should use tape recorders and phonographs, the telephone, radio and television, all means available to apprise people of the need for recreation and the opportunities that are afforded by the school recreation program.

B. *Visual.* This method is highly successful in the school recreation program. The following techniques have been used very satisfactorily. Presenting motion pictures of the recreation program in action is a dramatically convincing way of demonstrating the total scope of the program and the joy of participants. Slides, photographic displays and sketches, posters, placards and cartoons may be used in commercial buildings, school buildings, the city and school newspapers.

Exhibitions and demonstrations are effective in assembly programs, during the half-time of sports events, on television, and on other special occasions such as in parades and pageants. Contests and tournaments, trophies, certificates, plaques, ribbons, medals, and other awards all bring recognition to the program. Occasional clinics are helpful. Neat, informative bulletin boards attract attention.

C. *Printed.* Printed material, though expensive, is an excellent medium for promoting good public relations for the school recreation program. Pamphlets and leaflets, newsletters, handbooks, maps, charts, diagrams and annual reports may be directed to participants, to school authorities or to influential community members. Participants enjoy annuals and scrapbooks. Questionnaires and opinionnaires not only call attention to the recreation program but their results are often helpful in improving the program and in marshalling public support for it.

Public relations is the composite of *all* those things that tend to give the public an image of the program which one is trying to promote and for which understanding and support are sought. In the final analysis the job that is done must be the justification for its existence. We cannot afford to organize and supervise a school recreation program haphazardly. Every phase must be systematically studied and presented in order to present a lasting and proper image. Assistants must be carefully selected and instructed with regard to how they act. The attitudes of even the custodian, caretaker and secretary are greatly influential in creating an image for the recreation department.

Above all, we must create an awareness that recreation is essential to personality growth and mental and emotional stability, and that through recreation an individual finds opportunities for self-realization, social awareness, leadership, and followership. If we can develop this attitude we can be assured that we have developed satisfactory public relations.

Chapter 17

Review-View-Preview

As far back as Plato educators have implied that the aim of education should be to prepare man to use his leisure time in a worthy manner. Throughout the years prominent educators — Comenius, Locke, Basedow, Froebel, Pestalozzi, Rousseau — supported this contention. We have sketched in these pages the development of the idea that it is the school's responsibility to provide suitable recreation as one answer to the problem of educating man to use his leisure time profitably. Let us now review the growth of this idea in the United States.

THE PAST

Exacting demands for mere existence left the early American Colonials with very little leisure time. Life in the wilderness was so challenging that every able-bodied man and woman spent long hours at hard work. Hardships of all kinds — physical, economic, political, philosophical — discouraged expenditures of time or money for personal satisfaction, but these people were driven by motives much stronger than those of either survival or material success. Schools were somehow soon established, the curriculum consisting of reading, writing, arithmetic, and religion. School recreation at this time was completely unknown.

The change from handwork to machine and power tool production brought on by the Industrial Revolution resulted in unparalleled economic and social growth. This eventually brought about a complete change in man's methods of making a living, and indeed in all aspects of his life.

We have seen that in time the Dame and Kitchen schools gave way to the Latin Grammar Schools which later gave way to the Academies. Finally the Kalamazoo case paved the way for free public education, but it was not until the twentieth century that the use of leisure time became a problem or its consideration a possibility. Prior to this time, school recreation programs were certainly not planned; they just happened.

In these pages we have traced some of the milestones along the path of the development of school recreation, pausing to examine various beliefs regarding the meaning and value of play and noting the many benefits of recreation. We have maintained that a logical place for recreation

education is in the schools and have pointed out that the key to recreation's potential values lies in the kind of leadership provided. We have listed principles of recreational leadership and administration and have examined different aspects of programs: intramurals, clubs, special interests. Let us now take a look at contemporary forces which challenge us now and speculate on their future import.

THE PRESENT AND THE FUTURE

During the past few years, a number of unpredictable forces have radically altered our way of life and many of these are related to and intimately associated with changing trends in organized recreation.

Changing Attitudes

Interest in human welfare, comfort, and luxury has developed dramatically and there is now an ever-increasing, unprecedented desire for pleasurable activity. The need for increased recreation tends to keep pace with our ever-higher standard of living. Barring some unforeseen catastrophe, we can expect this trend to continue. We are told that we can look forward to a continuing increase in standards of living, annual incomes, cost of living, and amount of leisure time.

Until recently, man had no cause to concern himself with the possibility of overpopulating the earth. Now we recognize this as a major problem. It is predicted that the present three billion persons will double by the end of this century. With a continual expansion of population and its uneven distribution throughout the world, further and more complicated changes in our way of life will inevitably occur.

Mounting Tensions

The increasing tension between the "have" and "have-not" peoples of the earth is easily sensed and observed. The well-fed, well-clothed, well-housed, luxury loving minority are being challenged by the less fortunate majority. It is entirely possible that all major cities of the world may be reduced to radioactive rubble in which case society might revert to savagery.

A longer life, greater personal security, and more material comforts are looked upon as major promises for future happiness. These are desired by all men but only major economic adjustments can bring them about. Let us hope, however, that these occur within the philosophy that all men should earn what they receive for otherwise we can expect a general retardation in many phases of life.

The objective of education should be the improvement of society. We should attempt to make everybody somebody. These things are not probable unless we make it possible for all men to earn a decent living, secure adequate food, housing, clothing, and a dignified way of life. Every individual must be allowed, encouraged, and helped to enjoy whatever status he is capable of attaining for himself out of general striving as prescribed by a just and equitably enforced set of rules. Our goals must be set on improving the education, skills, ambitions, and desires of those who have been isolated by poverty and discrimination.

Changes in Work Habits

Automation has already created and will probably continue to create serious unemployment problems. It is currently eliminating 40,000 jobs per week in this country. Competition for employment will consequently increase and with this there may be growth of many borderline misfits.

It has been estimated that there will be more labor-saving inventions during the next twenty years than have been created in all recorded history. Job specialization will most likely continue to rise and become more complex while at the same time and, at an accelerated tempo, opportunities for the unskilled laborer will diminish. It is doubtful if we now know how to sustain a culture that does not depend upon work to give meaning to lives, but unless this problem is solved we will be engulfed with problems more vast than any nation has ever faced. The amount of leisure earned and forced upon tomorrow's citizens will be unprecedented. What is done with this time will result in man's growth and happiness or his destruction. We can anticipate automation to continue at an ever-increasing tempo. The result will be a concomitant shortening of the work day, work week, and work year. A thirty-hour work week, nine months per year, will probably not be uncommon within the next decade.

Tomorrow's Homes

Homes will soon be equipped with thermoelectric refrigerators, electro-luminiscent light, ultrasonic washing machines, full-wall stereo television screens, and hundreds of push-botton labor-saving devices. Home life has changed from covered wagons, a home on wheels, to the automobile, a room in motion. The impact of fast transportation is just now being realized. Mobility will most likely be a key factor in the development of homes in the future. To move is as natural to Americans as maintaining roots is to Europeans. Mobility makes possible a wide choice of pleasures. It is also compatible with our extremely fluid social structure. The architecture for mass leisure will require a kind of adaptability that assures privacy when it is needed, thus some rooms will come and go at the discretion of the occupants. A relaxed setting for a life of busy leisure will be required and designers will have to create an environment that will contain our mobility without restraining it.

Curriculum Changes

What will the future school curriculum be like? Undoubtedly there will be changes. We can not know what skills may be needed, but we are sure that everyone must be trained to cope with change. Since ultimate success is dependent on more than scholastic and technical mastery, future educational objectives will most likely emphasize the development of values, zeal, judgment, staying power, critical qualities of mind, durable qualities of character, resiliency, and other goals frequently ignored when schools are forced to develop crash programs.

Society has been wasteful of talent but the most damaging negligence has been in the handling of the might-have-beens. A great many of these dropouts, totaling approximately one million each year, become frustrated, antisocial, and rebellious. Their parents are generally undereducated, unskilled, and isolated by poverty and discrimination. It is not uncommon to find third generations on relief. Seldom do those now living in these pockets of poverty develop ambition or aspirations. They seldom develop salable skills. A real difficulty is to find suitable vocational tasks for uninspired, slow learners. Additional leisure tends to promote vandalism and foster many forms of personal and social misconduct. Organized school recreation programs can contribute to the elimination of this problem.

Curriculums must include education for the worthy use of leisure time: recreation education. Leisure time we shall have and its constructive use must not be left to chance. Those who now worry about delinquency, about the cost of welfare and policing agencies and about the cost of education have seen nothing in comparison to what can be expected unless we make *complete education* our major objective. We know that we now develop in each person only a fragment of what he could be. The aims of education and recreation are approximately the same; both are essential for the favorable growth and development of tomorrow's citizens.

DEVELOPMENT OF SCHOOL RECREATION

It is the school's responsibility to cultivate in students an interest in worthwhile activities. Recreation is an attitude of mind. Any interest can become recreation. Though other types of recreation have been mentioned throughout these pages and all recreational participation is important and desirable, active physical recreation has been stressed for this need is particularly acute in our society and will increase in the future. Active recreation affords joyous and exhilarating experiences for adventurous and restless young minds and bodies.

Recreation perhaps is one of the greatest of all sociological forces, and yet it provides an island for those wishing to escape. Through recreation pace can readily be changed from tensions and pressures. Recreation can be used as water when one is forced to prime his own pump. It can be a catalyst to effective and constructive living. Properly supervised, it can become a bridge for those having divergent cultural backgrounds. Organized recreation arrests ugly attitudes and contributes to good relationships.

Annual statistics now show that an increasing number of schools are establishing substantial budgets for recreational purposes. It seems safe to anticipate the continuing acceptance of recreational activities as an integral part of school life. Tomorrow's schools must certainly have tremendously expanded recreational programs. These will include sports, music, dance, crafts, art, interest groups of all kinds: photography, fishing and hunting, skiing and sailing, stamp collecting, painting, sculpture, ceramics, modeling, choral and instrumental groups, leathercraft and woodwork, nature study and scientific interests, foreign language, and the like. Recreation will make an impact on all education and education will come to encompass recreation. Together they will become the social force of every neighborhood. All our communities will become "cities of lighted schoolhouses" for purposes of wholesome recreation. It seems reasonable to assume that all available school facilities will eventually be used for recreational purposes, seven nights a week, on week ends, and during vacation periods. This will occur because an enlightened and concerned society will come to understand that recreational illiteracy cannot be tolerated and wholesome recreational interest can truly lead to the good life.

Appendix

RECREATION QUESTIONNAIRE

Name.. Address..

Class.. Club.............................. Phone..................

It is the college administration's objective to provide an extensive intramural program on campus. Participation in intramurals will not raise your I.Q., but it *has* been proved that it need not interfere with your academic status. Studies of this question have been made at leading universities. Sociologists, psychologists, educators, and doctors believe that active participation in sports and dance is so beneficial that they should be an everyday part of each person's life.

Every effort is being made to offer as many activities in our recreation program as you desire. If you wish to take part in any of the following and if there are enough others desiring this particular activity, the school will sponsor it.

Check only the activities in which you would like to participate.

Men's Activities
.... Badminton
.... Basketball
.... Handball
.... Soccer
.... Softball
.... Squash
.... Table Tennis
.... Tennis
.... Touch Football
.... Volleyball

Women's Activities
.... Archery
.... Badminton
.... Basketball
.... Field Hockey
.... Modern Dance
.... Softball
.... Speedball
.... Synchronized Swimming
.... Table Tennis
.... Tennis
.... Volleyball

Co-Recreational Clubs
.... Archery club
.... Badminton club
.... Bowling club
.... Horseback riding club
.... Ice skating club
.... Outing club
.... Recreational leadership club
.... Sailing club
.... Ski club
.... Social dance club
.... Square dance club
.... Swimming club

Social Activities
.... Beach Parties
.... Mountain trips
.... Picnics
.... Play Nights

Comments and other suggestions: ....

....

....

(Please return to the Recreation Director's office, Room .... Bldg. at your earliest convenience.)

LEADER'S SELF-EVALUATION CHECK LIST

	High to Low				
	5	4	3	2	1
1. Have I considered the needs of all members?					
2. Have I provided an adequate number and variety of activities?					
3. Have I divided the group adequately for maximum participation?					
4. Does my program allow for maximum skill development?					
5. Have I sufficiently helped those who need help most?					
6. Have I curtailed the movements of the over-active?					
7. Have I introduced new activities with enthusiasm?					
8. Have I fostered the development of cooperative attitudes?					
9. Did the participants have fun?					
10. Were the experiences participated in worthwhile?					
11. Did the experiences contribute to character development?					
12. Was there evidence in the participants of physical, mental, and social growth?					

Score of: 55–60 Excellent

48–54 Good

40–47 Average

34–39 Fair

38 and lower -- Poor

EVALUATION OF STUDENT LEADERS

Date _____

Student _____ Critic Observer _____

	High to Low				
	5	4	3	2	1
1. Personal Impression					
Dress _____					
Voice _____					
Posture _____					
Grooming _____					
Poise before the group _____					
Freedom from mannerisms _____					
2. Attitude					
Attendance _____					
Promptness _____					
Initiative _____					
Responses _____					
Enthusiasm _____					
Adjustment _____					
Resourcefulness _____					
Confidence _____					
Willingness to take criticism _____					
Professional characteristics _____					
3. Ability					
To control the group _____					
To plan _____					
To organize _____					
To follow through _____					
To evidence knowledge of activity ___					
To recognize individual differences __					
To arouse interest _____					
To use language appropriately ___					
4. Prediction					
Future expectations for the student __					

REMARKS: _____

HANDBALL ENTRY FORM
(Name of School)

Play Begins Tuesday, March 10, 1964

Rules and Regulations

1. All entries must be in the Intramural Office, P. E. 112, by Friday, March 6, 1964.

2. Official handball rules will govern tournament competition.

3. Each entrant is responsible for playing his match at the proper time.

4. First round matches will begin Tuesday, March 10.

5. Winners of each match must turn in the results to the U. R. A. office, P. E. 112, and post them on the bulletin board.

6. This will be a double elimination tournament.

OFFICIAL ENTRY BLANK

- -

Name _____ Phone _____

Address _____ City _____ Zone _____

My Doubles Partner _____ Phone _____

Address _____ City _____ Zone _____

Please accept my entry blank for the following events:

      Men's Singles   Men's Doubles

Partner's name must appear on this entry blank or doubles team will not be placed in the draw. Entrants will be responsible for notifying partners of scheduled matches.

135

Official Wrestling Entry Form
(Name of School)

Organization _____ Manager _____

Address _____ Phone No. _____

123 lb. Class   Phys. Exam. Date

Name: _____   _____

Alt. _____   _____

130 lb. Class

Name: _____   _____

Alt. _____   _____

137 lb. Class

Name: _____   _____

Alt. _____   _____

147 lb. Class

Name: _____   _____

Alt. _____   _____

157 lb. Class

Name: _____   _____

Alt. _____   _____

167 lb. Class

Name: _____   _____

Alt. _____   _____

177 lb. Class

Name: _____   _____

Alt. _____   _____

Unlimited Class

Name: _____   _____

Alt. _____   _____

TEAM SPORTS ENTRY BLANK
(Name of School)

Name of Team _____

Manager _____ Phone _____

Address _____

_____   _____
Sport   League

TEAM ROSTER

NAME (Type or Print)	Address	Phone
1.		
2.		
3.		
4.		
5.		
6.		
7.		
8.		
9.		
10.		
11.		
12.		
13.		
14.		
15.		

Managers: This entry blank must be registered in the University Recreation Office. All players must be listed on this roster before they are eligible to compete as a member of this team.

SINGLES AND DOUBLES ENTRY FORM
(Name of School)

Activity _____   Division _____

Entries Close _____   Play Begins _____

SINGLES

Name (PRINT last name first)	Address	Phone
1. _____	_____	_____
2. _____	_____	_____
3. _____	_____	_____
4. _____	_____	_____
5. _____	_____	_____
6. _____	_____	_____
7. _____	_____	_____
8. _____	_____	_____

DOUBLES

Names (PRINT last name first)	Address	Phone
1. _____	_____	_____
2. _____	_____	_____
3. _____	_____	_____
4. _____	_____	_____
5. _____	_____	_____

TRACK ENTRY BLANK
(Name of School)

Organization _____   Manager _____

60 yard Dash

1. _____

2. _____

100 yard Dash

1. _____

2. _____

300 yard Dash

1. _____

2. _____

3/4 Mile Run

1. _____

2. _____

70 yard High Hurdles

1. _____

2. _____

70 yard Low Hurdles

1. _____

2. _____

440 yard Relay

1. _____

2. _____

3. _____

4. _____

Pole Vault

1. _____

2. _____

High Jump

1. _____

2. _____

Broad Jump

1. _____

2. _____

Shot Put

1. _____

2. _____

Discus

1. _____

2. _____

880 Relay

1. _____

2. _____

3. _____

4. _____

PLEASE PRINT ALL NAMES.
(Last name first.) Entry deadline
is Wednesday, April 16th. Contestants may enter but two individual
events plus the relays. Only one
team from each unit can be entered
in each relay event.

ELIGIBILITY LIST
(Name of School)

Organization _____ Manager _____

Address _____ Phone _____

PRINT THE FULL NAMES ALPHABETICALLY
WITH THE LAST NAME FIRST

1. _____   21. _____

2. _____   22. _____

3. _____   23. _____

4. _____   24. _____

5. _____   25. _____

6. _____   26. _____

7. _____   27. _____

8. _____   28. _____

9. _____   29. _____

10. _____   30. _____

11. _____   31. _____

12. _____   32. _____

13. _____   33. _____

14. _____   34. _____

15. _____   35. _____

16. _____   36. _____

17. _____   37. _____

18. _____   38. _____

19. _____   39. _____

20. _____   40. _____

PROTEST
(Name of School)

Notice: All protests, except those concerning use of ineligible players, must be submitted in writing to the Intramural Director within 24 hours following the disputed contest.

Sport _____   Date _____

Team Protesting _____   Opponents _____

Date of Game _____   Time _____ Place _____

Score of Game _____   Officials _____

SUMMARY OF PROTEST

_____

_____

_____

_____

_____

_____

_____

_____

_____

_____

_____

_____

_____

_____

_____

Manager _____ Organization _____ Phone _____

PROTEST SUMMARY RECORD
(Name of School)

Date of Hearing _____

Team Protesting _____   Represented by _____

Opponents _____   Represented by _____

Board Members Present: Witnesses Present:

1.   1.

2.   2.

3.   3.

4.   4.

5.   5.

DECISION OF BOARD

_____

_____

_____

REASONS FOR DECISION

_____

_____

_____

_____

_____

_____

_____

_____

_____   _____
Protest Committee Chairman   Secretary

REPORT OF INJURY
(Name of School)

Name _____   Phone _____

Address _____   Date _____

Activity _____   Time _____

Place where accident occurred _____

Cause and nature of injury _____

_____

_____

Type of first aid given _____

_____

_____

Disposition _____

_____

_____

WITNESSES

_____   _____

_____   _____

CAUSE OF ACCIDENT

_____ Poor equipment   _____ Poor playing surface

_____ Bad judgment, carelessness   _____ Poor illumination

_____ Poor skill   _____ Inadequate space

Other (describe) _____

_____

_____

_____   _____
Person in Charge   Person Making Report

BASKETBALL SCORE SHEET
(Name of School)

League _____ Gym _____ Date _____

TEAM (SUMMARY

	Name	No.	Individual Scores	Fouls	FG	FT	FC	TP
F								
F								
F								
F								
C								
C								
G								
G								
G								
G								

TEAM (SUMMARY

	Name	No.	Individual Scores	Fouls	FG	FT	FC	TP
F								
F								
F								
F								
C								
C								
G								
G								
G								
G								

Running Score:

	Time out	1 2 3 4 5 6 7 8 9 10 11 12 13 14 15 16 17 18 19 20
1 2 3 4 5		21 22 23 24 25 26 27 28 29 30 31 32 33 34 35 36 37 38 39 40
		41 42 43 44 45 46 47 48 49 50
	Time out	1 2 3 4 5 6 7 8 9 10 11 12 13 14 15 16 17 18 19 20
		21 22 23 24 25 26 27 28 29 30 31 32 33 34 35 36 37 38 39 40
		41 42 43 44 45 46 47 48 49 50

Referee _____ Umpire _____ Scorer _____

Attendance _____   Round _____

DIVING SCORE CARD
(Name of School)

DIVING SCORE CARD   Name: _____   Organization: _____

No.	Group	Dive No.	Dive	Judges Awards	Total	Degree of Difficulty	Total Points
1							
2							
3							
4							
5							
6							
7							
8							

Softball Score Sheet
(Name of School)

Teams _____ vs _____

	Pos.	1	2	3	4	5	6	7	8	9
	HR									
	Pos.	1	2	3	4	5	6	7	8	9
	HR									

Date _____

Time _____

Field _____

SCORING SYMBOLS

	Single
	Double
	Triple
	Home Run
K	Strikeout
S	Stolen Base
B	Base on Balls
H	Hit by Pitch
W	Wild Pitch
P	Passed Ball
Bk	Balk Run
FC	Fielders Choice
E	Error

POSITION NUMBERS

1	Pitcher
2	Catcher
3	1st Base
4	2nd Base
5	3rd Base
6	Short Stop
7	Left Field
8	Center Field
9	Right Field

OFFICIALS

_____

Teams	1	2	3	4	5	6	7	8	9	Total

TAG FOOTBALL
(Name of School)

Team:

Team:

Position	Touchdowns	Extra Points	Safeties	Field Goals
LE				
LG				
C				
RG				
RE				
QB				
RHB				
LHB				
FB				

Position	Touchdowns	Extra Points	Safeties	Field Goals
LE				
LG				
C				
RG				
RE				
QB				
RHB				
LHB				
FB				

Teams	1st Half	2nd Half	Final Score

Date:
Field: Time:
Referee:
Umpire:
Linesman:

Tennis Score Sheet
(Name of School)

Date: _____ Time: _____ Court: _____ Official: _____

Team _____ vs. Team _____

SINGLES

Set Scores			Name	vs	Name	Set Scores		
1	2	3				1	2	3
				vs				
				vs				
				vs				

DOUBLES

Set Scores			Names	vs	Names	Set Scores		
1	2	3				1	2	3
				vs				
				vs				

Track and Field Master Score Sheet
(Name of School)

Organization	60 yard Dash	70 yard High Hurdles	3/4 Mile Run	100 yard Dash	70 yard Low Hurdles	300 yard Run	High Jump	Broad Jump	Shot Put	440 yard Relay	Pole Vault	Discus	880 yard Relay	Total

Volleyball Score Sheet
(Name of School)

Date _____ Court _____ Time _____

TEAM

LF	
CF	
RF	
LB	
CB	
RB	

TEAM

LF	
CF	
RF	
LB	
CB	
RB	

GAME I

1 2 3 4 5 6 7 8	Score
9 10 11 12 13 14 15 16	
17 18 19 20 21	

GAME II

1 2 3 4 5 6 7 8	Score
9 10 11 12 13 14 15 16	
17 18 19 20 21	

GAME III

1 2 3 4 5 6 7 8	Score
9 10 11 12 13 14 15 16	
17 18 19 20 21	

GAME I

1 2 3 4 5 6 7 8	Score
9 10 11 12 13 14 15 16	
17 18 19 20 21	

GAME II

1 2 3 4 5 6 7 8	Score
9 10 11 12 13 14 15 16	
17 18 19 20 21	

GAME III

1 2 3 4 5 6 7 8	Score
9 10 11 12 13 14 15 16	
17 18 19 20 21	

Winner: _____   Referee: _____

FIELD EVENT RECORD
(Name of School)

Event: _____ Date: _____ Time: _____

Name	Organization	1	2	3	4	5	6	7

FINAL RESULTS -- Distance or Height   Judges

Name	Organization		
1.			Chief:
2.			Judge:
3.			Judge:
4.			Retriever:

151

Track Event Record
(Name of School)

Event: _____ Date: _____ Time: _____

Lane	Contestant's Name	Number	Organization	Position Finished

Winners	Number	Organization	Time
1.			
2.			
3.			
4.			
5.			

ACTIVITY SUMMARY
(Name of School)

Activity _____ Semester _____

Date Activity Started _____ Date of Finals _____

Number of Participants: Number of Teams Participating:

    Co-Recreational Division _____   Co-Recreational Division _____

    Dormitory Division _____   Dormitory Division _____

    Fraternity Division _____   Fraternity Division _____

    Sorority Division _____   Sorority Division _____

    Independent Division _____   Independent Division _____

           Total _____   Total _____

Number of New Participants: Dormitory _____ Co-Recreation _____

    Fraternity _____ Sorority _____ Independent _____

	No. Games Scheduled	No. Forfeits	No. Games Played
Co-Recreational Division			
Dormitory Division			
Fraternity Division			
Sorority Division			
Independent Division			
Total			

Number of Teams Dropped: Dormitory_____ Co-Recreation _____

    Fraternity_____ Sorority_____ Independent _____

Number of Officials Used: _____ Total Salary of Officials: _____

Number of Major Injuries: _____ List Type: _____

_____

_____

CHAMPIONS

Dormitory_____ Fraternity_____

Co-Recreational _____ Sorority _____

Independent _____ Campus _____

REMARKS

_____

_____

_____

Submitted by: _____

EXTRAMURAL RECREATION ASSOCIATION
(Tentative Draft of Constitution)

ARTICLE I
Name

The name of this organization shall be The Southern California College Extramural Recreation Association.

ARTICLE II
Purpose

The purpose of this Association shall be:

Section I   To promote greater interest in extramural recreational activities.

Section II   To provide student leaders an opportunity for personal and professional growth through participation and administration of such a program.

Section III To develop a feeling of inter-institutional unity and good fellowship through social, recreational, and educational programs sponsored by this Association.

Section IV   To extend the privileges and values of intergroup participation through association-sponsored playoffs, meets, and tournaments conducted in the best interests of its participants.

ARTICLE III
Membership

Membership shall be open to all students in four-year colleges and universities in Southern California which are officially accredited and bona fide collegiate institutions of higher learning, and which express desire to participate in its activities and abide by its rules.

ARTICLE IV
Dues

The dues shall be .... per year, payable to the Association treasurer prior to official entry into the Association program by September 30th of each year. Failure to pay will constitute reason for rejection in Association activities.

ARTICLE V
The Representative Council

The Representative Council shall be composed of one faculty representative and one student representative from each member college of the Association.

ARTICLE VI
Officers

The officers of this Association shall be elected annually from the ranks of the Representative Assembly at the last meeting in the spring semester, and shall be as follows: Chairman, Vice-Chairman, Secretary, and Treasurer. Furthermore, the officers of this Association shall be elected from the ranks of the *student* representatives.

ARTICLE VII
Committees

Section I　　The standing committees with respective chairmen shall be appointed by the Association chairman with the approval of the Representative Council and shall consist of the following: awards, scheduling, rules, publicity, protest and forfeiture, insurance and liability, and such other committees that are deemed essential by the Representative Council. All standing committees shall be composed of student representatives except as stated in Article VIII and Article II, Section VII (By-laws).

Section II　　There shall be a nominating committee of three members appointed by the chairman who shall submit a slate of officers for the ensuing year one week prior to the date of the final meeting.

ARTICLE VIII
Faculty Advisors

Each participating college shall be represented by a regular faculty member whose duties it shall be to see that all matters pertaining to this program are conducted in the best interest of the students and administrators of all member institutions. Faculty members shall automatically become ex-officio advisory members to any standing committee where the appointed student chairman is from the same institution as the faculty advisor.

ARTICLE IX
Meetings

Regular meetings of the Representative Council shall be held at stated intervals as jointly agreed upon by the council.

ARTICLE X
Amendments

The Constitution may be amended by a two-thirds vote of all members of the Representative Council. The proposed amendment must be published for the Association at least one week prior to the meeting.

ARTICLE XI
Voting Powers

Final action on all matters pertaining to the Association shall be determined by a two-thirds majority vote of its members. Each member of the Representative Council shall have one vote and shall also be granted the privilege of an absentee ballot in case of absence.

By-Laws

ARTICLE I
Duties of Officers

Section I   The chairman shall preside at all meetings and conduct them by a formal order of business.

Section II   The vice-chairman shall perform the duties of the chairman in his absence.

Section III The secretary shall notify members of meetings of the Association. He shall keep a list of all member colleges with representatives on the various standing committees and shall keep a written record of all meetings.

Section IV   The treasurer shall receive, hold, and pay out all moneys of the Association subject to the order of the president. He shall keep a written account of all money received and paid out, and shall make a formal report to the Association at the last meeting of the school year.

ARTICLE II
Function of Committees

Section I   The function of all committees shall be to investigate and to make recommendations to the Representative Council. The power to make final decisions on all committee findings shall reside with the Representative Council.

Section II   The publicity committee shall be in charge of all promotional activities of the organization.

Section III   The awards committee shall determine all matters pertaining to an equitable and reasonable system of awards.

Section IV   The rules and regulations committee shall formulate a set of rules and regulations deemed essential to the effective operation of this Association.

Section V   The scheduling committee shall draw up a schedule of events and set the time, place, and dates of the same in all intercollegiate playoffs or tournaments.

Section VI   The protest and forfeiture committee shall formally consider all bona-fide grievances which involve infractions of the rules and regulations and shall recommend appropriate action for same.

Section VII   The insurance and liability committee (composed of faculty members) shall be responsible for investigating all the problems of liability and defining the areas of responsibility and they shall inform the participants and Representative Council of the same.

Section VIII   The nominating committee shall submit a panel of officers consisting of at least two members for each officer one week before the last meeting of the spring semester.

Section IX   All standing committees with the exception of the insurance and liability committee shall be composed of students appointed by the Association chairman. Each standing committee shall have one representative faculty member assigned to it for the purpose of performing ex-officio advisory functions as defined in Article VIII (Faculty Advisors).

Bibliography

1. American Association for Health, Physical Education and Recreation. *Recruitment of Recreation Personnel.* Washington, D. C.: National Education Association, 1959.
2. ANDREWS, GLADYS; JEANETTE SOURBORN, AND ELSA SCHNEIDER. *Physical Education for Today's Boys and Girls.* Boston: Allyn and Bacon, Inc., 1960.
3. ANGELL, ROBERT C. *The Campus.* New York: D. Appleton and Company, 1928.
4. BEEMAN, HARRIS F., AND JAMES H. HUMPHREY. *Intramural Sports: A Text and Study Guide.* Dubuque: Wm. C. Brown Company Publishers, 1954.
5. BERNARD, HAROLD W. *Toward Better Personal Adjustment.* New York: McGraw-Hill Book Company, Inc., 1951.
6. BOGARDUS, EMORY S. *Fundamentals of Social Psychology.* New York: Appleton-Century-Crofts, Inc., 1942.
7. BORST, EVELYNE, AND ELMER D. MITCHELL. *Social Games for Recreation.* 2d ed. New York: The Ronald Press, 1959.
8. BRAMMELL, ROY. *Intramural and Interscholastic Athletics.* Washington: U. S. Department of the Interior Monograph, No. 27, 1932.
9. BRIGHTBILL, CHARLES K., AND HAROLD D. MEYER. *Recreation, Text and Readings.* New York: Prentice-Hall, Inc., 1953.
10. .... *Recreation Administration.* Englewood Cliffs: Prentice-Hall, Inc., 1956.
11. BRIGHTBILL, CHARLES K. *Man and Leisure.* Englewood Cliffs: Prentice-Hall, Inc., 1961.

12. BRUBAKER, JOHN S., AND RUBY WILLIS. *Higher Education in Transition.* New York: Harper and Brothers Publishers, 1958.

13. BUTLER, GEORGE D. *Introduction to Community Education.* New York: McGraw-Hill Book Company, Inc., 1959.

14. CALLERY, JOHN. "Intramural Program for a Small High School," *Athletic Journal,* 30-60, September, 1949.

15. CARLSON, REYNOLD E., THEODORE R. DEPPE, AND JANET R. MACLEAN. *Recreation in American Life.* Belmont: Wadsworth Publishing Company, Inc., 1963.

16. CHRISTENSON, IRV. "Building Good Intramural Sports Programs," *School Management,* 13:86 (November, 1943).

17. CORBALLY, JOHN E.; T. J. JENSON; AND FREDERICK STAUB. *Educational Administration: The Secondary School.* Boston: Allyn and Bacon, Inc., 1961.

18. CORBIN, H. DAN. *Recreation Leadership.* 2d ed. Englewood Cliffs, N. J.: Prentice-Hall, Inc., 1959.

19. DANFORD, HOWARD G. *Creative Leadership in Recreation.* Boston: Allyn and Bacon, 1964.

20. DANFORD, HOWARD G. (Ed.). *School Recreation, National Conference Report.* Washington: AAHPER, 1960.

21. DEWEY, JOHN. *Human Nature and Conduct.* New York: Henry Holt and Company, 1922.

22. DIMOCK, HEDLEY S., AND HARLEIGH B. TRECKER. *The Supervision of Group Work and Recreation.* New York: Association Press, 1949.

23. DRAPER, EDGAR MARIAN, AND GEORGE MIMMS SMITH. *Intramural Athletics and Play Days.* New York: A. S. Barnes and Company, Inc., 1930.

24. DUNCAN, MARGARET M., AND RALPH H. JOHNSON. *Introduction to Physical Education, Health Education, and Recreation.* New Jersey: Prentice-Hall, Inc., 1959.

25. EBY, FREDERICK, AND CHARLES FLINN ARROWOOD. *The Development of Modern Education.* New York: Prentice-Hall, Inc., 1945.

26. EDDY, EDWARD D. *The College Influence on Student Character.* Washington: American Council on Education, 1957.

27. EDWARDS, NEWTON. *The Courts and the Public Schools.* Chicago: University of Chicago Press, 1940.

28. FORSYTHE, CHARLES E., AND RAY O. DUNCAN. *Administration of Physical Education.* New York: Prentice-Hall, Inc., 1951.

29. GEYER, FORREST. "A Tentative Intramural Program for John Marshall Junior High School." Unpublished Master's project, University of Southern California, 1953.

30. HALL, J. TILLMAN. *Dance, A Complete Guide to Social, Folk and Square Dancing.* Belmont: Wadsworth Publishing Company, Inc., 1963.

31. HAVEL, RICHARD C., AND EMERY W. SEYMOUR. *Administration of Health, Physical Education, and Recreation for Schools.* New York: The Ronald Press, 1961.

32. HOLMES, MALCOLM H. *Conducting an Amateur Orchestra.* Cambridge: Harvard University Press, 1951.

33. HUGHES, WILLIAM L., ESTHER FRENCH, AND NELSON G. LEHSTON. *The Administration of Physical Education.* New York: The Ronald Press, 1962.
34. HUTCHINSON, JOHN L. *Principles of Recreation.* New York: A. S. Barnes and Company, 1949.
35. JENNY, JOHN H. *Physical Education, Health Education, and Recreation.* New York: The Macmillan Company, 1961.
36. KAPLAN, MAX. *Leisure in America.* New York: John Wiley and Sons, Inc., 1960.
37. KERR, WALTER. *The Decline of Pleasure.* New York: Simon and Schuster, 1962.
38. KRAUS, RICHARD. *Recreation Leader's Handbook.* New York: McGraw-Hill Book Company, Inc., 1955.
39. LANDECK, BEATRICE. *Children and Music.* New York: William Sloane Associates, Inc., 1952.
40. LANGTON, CLAIR V. *Handbook of Intramural Sports.* Eugene: Oregon State College-Publication, 1930.
41. LEAVITT, NORMAN M., AND HARTLEY D. PRICE. *Intramural and Recreational Sports for Men and Women.* New York: A. S. Barnes and Company, 1949.
42. LEE, JOSEPH. *The Normal Course in Play.* New York: A. S. Barnes and Company, 1926.
43. *Leisure and the Schools.* Washington: American Association for Health, Physical Education, and Recreation, 1961.
44. LEONHARD, CHARLES. *Recreation Through Music.* New York: A. S. Barnes and Company, 1952.
45. Life Nature Library. *The Earth.* New York: Time Incorporated, 1962.
46. LIPOVETZ, FERD JOHN. *Recreation.* Minneapolis: Burgess Publishing Company, 1950.
47. LOKEN, NEWT, AND OTIS DYPWICK. *Cheerleading and Marching Bands.* New York: A. S. Barnes and Company, 1945.
48. LOKKA, ALFRED B. "A Guide for the Administration of an Intramural Program at the Secondary Level." Unpublished Master's project, University of Southern California, 1951.
49. McCONATHY, OSBOURNE. *Music for Early Childhood.* Sacramento: California State Department of Education, 1960.
50. MEANS, LOUIS E. *The Organization and Administration of Intramural Sports.* St. Louis: The C. V. Mosby Company, 1952.
51. Metropolitan Recreation and Youth Services Council. *The Next Ten Years.* Los Angeles, 1959.
52. MEYER, HAROLD D., AND CHARLES K. BRIGHTBILL. *Community Recreation.* Englewood Cliffs: Prentice-Hall, Inc., 1959.
53. .... *State Recreation: Organization and Administration.* New York: A. S. Barnes and Company, 1950.
54. MILLER, NORMAN P., AND DUANE M. ROBINSON. *The Leisure Age.* Belmont: Wadsworth Publishing Company, 1963.

55. Mitchell, Elmer D. *Intramural Athletics*. New York: A. S. Barnes and Company, 1925.

56. .... *Intramural Sports*. New York: A. S. Barnes and Company, 1939.

57. Mitchell, Elmer D., and Bernard S. Mason. *The Theory of Play*. New York: A. S. Barnes and Company, 1948.

58. Mulhern, James. *A History of Education*. New York: The Ronald Press, 1946.

59. Myers, Louise Kifer. *Teaching Children Music in the Elementary School*. New York: Prentice-Hall, Inc., 1950.

60. Nash, Jay B. *Physical Education: Interpretation and Objective*. Dubuque, Iowa: Wm. C. Brown Company Publishers, 1963.

61. Neumeyer, Martin H., and Esther S. Neumeyer. *Leisure and Recreation*. 3d ed. New York: The Ronald Press Co., 1959.

62. Rice, Emmett A. *A Brief History of Physical Education*. New York: A. S. Barnes and Company, 1926.

63. Rice, Thurman B., and Fred V. Hein. *Living*. Chicago: Scott Foresman and Company, 1954.

64. Sargent, S. Stansfeld. *The Basic Teachings of the Great Psychologists*. Philadelphia: The Blakiston Company, 1944.

65. Slavon, S. R. *Recreation and the Total Personality*. New York: Association Press, 1946.

66. Smalling, Ray. "Complete Intramural Program," *Scholastic Coach*, 19:51 (September, 1949).

67. Smith, Julian W. *Outdoor Education for American Youth*. Washington, D. C.: Washington Association for Health, Physical Education and Recreation, 1957.

68. Tague, Jean R. "Formula for Developing Leaders." Unpublished term paper, University of Southern California, 1962.

69. Thorpe, Louis P. *Psychological Foundations of Personality*. New York: McGraw-Hill Book Company, Inc., 1938.

70. Thorpe, Louis P. *Child Psychology and Development*. New York: The Ronald Press, 1955.

71. *The Machine at War*. Chicago: Wilson Sporting Goods Company, 1945.

72. Voltmer, Edward, and Arthur Esslinger. *Organization and Administration of Physical Education*. New York: A. S. Crofts and Company, 1938.

73. Voltmer, Carl D.; Thomas Scott; and Vernon Lapp. *The Intramural Handbook*. Minneapolis: Burgess Publishing Company, 1940.

74. Waske, Paul R. "A Study of Intramural Sports Participation and Scholastic Achievement." *Research Quarterly*, May, 1940.

75. Wrenn, C. Gilbert, and D. L. Harley. *Time on Their Hands*. Washington: American Council on Education, 1941.

Index